A MAJORITY OF ONE

A Majority of One

A COMEDY BY **Leonard Spigelgass**

RANDOM HOUSE • NEW YORK

To my grandmother

A MAJORITY OF ONE *was first presented by The Theatre Guild and Dore Schary at the Sam S. Shubert Theatre, New York City, on February 16, 1959, with the following cast:*
(*In order of appearance*)

MRS. RUBIN	Mae Questel
MRS. JACOBY	Gertrude Berg
ALICE BLACK	Ina Balin
JEROME BLACK	Michael Tolan
KOICHI ASANO	Cedric Hardwicke
LADY PASSENGER	Selma Halpern
EDDIE	Marc Marno
NOKETI	Sahomi Tachibana
HOUSE BOY	Arsenio Trinidad
AYAKO ASANO	Kanna Ishii
TATESHI	Tsuruko Kobayashi
MAID	Yasuko Adachi
CAPTAIN NORCROSS	Barnard Hughes
CHAUFFEUR	Arsenio Trinidad

Directed by Dore Schary

Associate producer, Philip Langner

Production designed and lighted by Donald Oenslager

Costumes by Motley

SYNOPSIS OF SCENES

Act One

Scene 1. Mrs. Jacoby's apartment in Brooklyn. A late afternoon in May.

Scenes 2, 3 and 4. The promenade deck of the *S.S. General Wood*, during the two-week voyage to Japan.

Act Two

Scene 1. The Black's home in Tokyo. August.

Scene 2. Mr. Asano's home in Tokyo. A half-hour later.

Act Three

Scene 1. The Blacks' home. Two hours later.

Scene 2. Mrs. Jacoby's home in Brooklyn. Two months later.

ACT ONE

"Any man more right than his neighbors, constitutes a majority of one."

Henry David Thoreau

The scene: A late afternoon in May. The living room of MRS.
BERTHA JACOBY'S *apartment in Brooklyn. The furnishings are
the cherished remnants of a large apartment compressed into a
small one. At stage left is a sofa covered in a blue print. Below
it is a coffee table, and to the right of that, a small hassock. Far
left is a small table. Up left is a sideboard. Stage right is a
dining table and three chairs. Up right is a breakfront on which
are framed photographs of Sam and David Jacoby, flanked by
a vase of flowers and a small American flag. A window, covered
by lace curtains, is stage right. A door from the apartment into
the building hallway is up center. Straight chairs are on either
side of it. Up left is a swinging door leading into the kitchen
and down left is the door to the bedroom. Many pictures are
hung on the walls, including those of* MRS. JACOBY'S *parents in
large, old-fashioned oval frames over the breakfront.*

At rise: The stage is empty. In the kitchen BERTHA JACOBY *is
singing as she prepares dinner amid the rattle of pots and pans.*
MRS. ESSIE RUBIN *enters, carrying an ice bucket and her purse.
She is sixtyish and wears a youthful black dress with blue trim.*

MRS. RUBIN   Bertha?

MRS. JACOBY (*Offstage*)   Essie? I'll be right there. (MRS. RUBIN *takes a piece of candy from a dish on the table*) Help yourself to some candy.

MRS. RUBIN (*Biting into candy*)   Uhh—maple walnut.
(*She swallows with a grimace as* MRS. JACOBY *comes in from the kitchen.* MRS. JACOBY *is in her late fifties, well held-together, with a clean face that has known many woes but remains cheerful. She is wearing a good black dress and a print apron*)

MRS. JACOBY   Be careful of the ones on the right, Essie. Nuts—and you hate them.

MRS. RUBIN   I already got stuck. So here's the ice bucket you wanted.

MRS. JACOBY   Thanks. I don't know what's with my Frigidaire. (*Noticing the bucket*) Stunning!

MRS. RUBIN   My son gave it to me for Christmas. From B. Altman.

MRS. JACOBY   It's a very practical present. I'll empty it and give it back.

MRS. RUBIN   No, no. Lend it. It'll make an impression.

MRS. JACOBY   On my daughter and son-in-law I need to make an impression?

MRS. RUBIN Mind if I sit down and have a Parliament?
(*She takes one from her purse and lights it*)

MRS. JACOBY Essie, every day you change your brand.

MRS. RUBIN I've been experimenting with filter tips.

MRS. JACOBY The best filter tip is—don't smoke.

MRS. RUBIN I got the monkey on my back.

MRS. JACOBY So what is it you want to tell me, Essie? Essie so
what do you want to tell me?

MRS. RUBIN Nothing.

MRS. JACOBY With a new home permanent on your head and
Fifth Avenue Red on your nails—nothing is cooking? So?

MRS. RUBIN So, the Bernsteins have this cousin in from Cleve-
land. We're all going to have dinner at Longchamps, then
take in a show.

MRS. JACOBY You've already met him?

MRS. RUBIN No, but the Bernsteins rave. He's retired from the
real estate business—a widower with a nice couple a dollars
and he's got four sons—all married.

MRS. JACOBY He's healthy?

5

MRS. RUBIN   Like a horse! Except for a small heart condition and he can't eat cholesterol.

MRS. JACOBY   Essie, you'll have your hands full with a diet.

MRS. RUBIN   I got to catch him first. I'm going to wear my blue fox stole and that dress I got down at your place.

MRS. JACOBY   I wish you'd taken another selection. That number is for a figure like—

MRS. RUBIN   Listen, I may not be Marilyn Monroe, but I don't happen to go for matronly clothes like some people.

MRS. JACOBY   Essie, I'm not a spring chicken.
   (*The door buzzer sounds*)

MRS. RUBIN   You may be willing to give up the sponge, but I'm not!

MRS. JACOBY   (*Hurrying to door*)   So good luck, darling. (*She opens the door to admit her daughter, ALICE, a very pretty girl in her middle twenties, dressed in a smart suit. Behind her is her husband, JEROME BLACK, who is in his middle thirties, intense, handsome, and self-possessed. He is wearing Ivy League clothes and carries a traveling bag and an attaché case, which he puts down as he enters*) Hello, Alice!

ALICE   Hello, Mama!

6

MRS. JACOBY Jerry!

JERRY Hello, Mama! How are you?

ALICE Mama, let me look at you. My goodness, you look young as ever. What's your secret?

MRS. JACOBY The same—hot water with lemon. You look a little tired, Alice.

ALICE I won't after I've had a bath.

MRS. JACOBY Let me fill my eyes with you, Jerry!

JERRY Beginning tomorrow, *I'm* going on a diet of hot water and lemon.

ALICE Hello, Mrs. Rubin. Jerry, you know Mrs. Rubin.

JERRY Certainly. Nice to see you again.
    (*They shake hands*)

MRS. RUBIN Likewise.

MRS. JACOBY How was your trip from Washington?

JERRY We ran into a headwind. Kind of bumpy.
    (*He picks up the bags and crosses to the bedroom door*)

MRS. JACOBY You flew?

ALICE   Yes, Mama. But we didn't tell you.

MRS. JACOBY   I'm glad I didn't know. How's your folks, Jerry?

JERRY   Booming. We're taking you to dinner there tomorrow night.

MRS. JACOBY   We'll see. Take a drink, darling. And take some ice from Essie's beautiful ice bucket she lent me.

ALICE   It's nice to have such thoughtful neighbors.

MRS. RUBIN   Maybe she wouldn't have for long.

MRS. JACOBY   Essie's thinking of moving out of Brooklyn.

MRS. RUBIN   To Manhattan. An apartment hotel. Costs a little more, but my son says it's worth it to get into a decent neighborhood again.

ALICE   What's wrong with this one?

MRS. RUBIN   Take a walk around Nostrand Avenue and you'll see. That element is moving in. The place is full of them.

JERRY   (*Quietly*) What element, Mrs. Rubin?

MRS. RUBIN   You know what I have reference to. Colored. Also Puerto Ricans.

8

MRS. JACOBY (*Entering and going to* ALICE *with a glass of soda*) You want, Essie? I have plenty.

MRS. RUBIN No, thanks. I'm saving up my appetite for a martini. I really got to get on my bicycle. (*To* ALICE) Oh, please thank your husband for a very stimulating conversation. Good-bye.

MRS. JACOBY Good-bye.

ALICE Good-bye.

(MRS. RUBIN *goes out*)

MRS. JACOBY So Essie isn't here. Now we can talk. You got something to tell me? Alice.

ALICE Yes, Mama, but I want Jerry to be here with me when I do.

MRS. JACOBY Maybe Jerry doesn't have to be here? Maybe your mama's a fortune teller? (*Looking at* ALICE's *figure*) January? December? I'm going to be a grandmother, Alice, yes?

ALICE (*Laughing*) No, Mama.

MRS. JACOBY (*Disappointed*) Did you go to see the doctor?

ALICE Yes, Mama. It's all right.

MRS. JACOBY You don't need an operation?

ALICE No. He gave me a series of exercises.

MRS. JACOBY Exercises? That's the new way?!

ALICE And lots of pills.

MRS. JACOBY (*Turns and takes candles from sideboard*) What you need is lots of *rest*.

ALICE *You* should talk! Mama, you're the one who should take it easy. Why did you take that job?

MRS. JACOBY A part-time job. A couple days a week.

ALICE Part-time or full-time, you still have to travel on the subway in the rush hour and stand on your feet all day. You know I worry about you.

MRS. JACOBY (*Placing plates on the table*) You don't have to, darling. What—you think I'm selling dresses in a bargain basement someplace? It's a lovely shop with fluorescent lights and air conditioning. I even get a coffee break.
(*She turns to get silver from the breakfront*)

ALICE I still don't like it.

MRS. JACOBY I like to keep busy. And besides, it takes a little financial burden off you and that makes me feel good.

ALICE Mama, never say that. If I worked all my life, I could never—

MRS. JACOBY (*Placing the silver on the table*) Sha-a-a. Alice, you don't mind if I ask you something? Do you know what was last Thursday?

ALICE Yes, Mama. It was David's *Jahrtzeit*. I didn't forget.

MRS. JACOBY (*Taking three glasses from the breakfront and placing them on the table*) Sixteen years he's gone. Remember the day he was drafted, and we took him to the subway station? (*Pulling herself together*) You know what I forgot! The napkins. For supper I made just what Jerry likes—a pot roast—not greasy—I know how he doesn't like greasy— potato *kugel*, peas and carrots (*She takes napkins from the small table and goes back to the dining table*) And, with my economy lemon icebox cake, I'm giving Jerry cream with his coffee!

ALICE Cream? After meat, Mama?

MRS. JACOBY I've been watching the television commercials and I got to live modern!
   (*She places the napkins*)

ALICE Jerry doesn't really mind.

MRS. JACOBY I know Jerry likes cream in his coffee. His family never kept kosher. Sometimes I wonder why *I* keep it up. But I think I know the answer. Remember Papa's joke? "I'm glad I don't like spinach because if I liked it I'd eat it and I hate it." Well, that's me. Sit. (ALICE *laughs*) So tell me Jerry's news already.

ALICE   All I can tell you is that Jerry's got a big promotion.

MRS. JACOBY   Leave it to Jerry. Like Papa always said, "He'll be an ambassador someday." By Papa, he was already an ambassador. I can just see Papa with his pinochle friends, saying, "My son the ambassador is now in France." Your Papa was some liar when it came to Jerry. Poor Papa. (ALICE *moves to sit beside her on the sofa. They touch foreheads for a brief, tender second, then* MRS. JACOBY *pats* ALICE's *cheek*) So—you know what you need? Go wash your face and comb your hair and put on a little more lipstick. I like that color. What is it?

ALICE   Revlon's Persian Melon. I'll give it to you.

MRS. JACOBY   No, for me I like better Bachelor's Carnation.

ALICE   What are you going to wear tomorrow night to Jerry's folks'?

MRS. JACOBY   Look how I forgot! I have a very important Sisterhood meeting. It's the committee on means and ways and I'm chairlady.

ALICE   Well, I'm afraid somebody else will have to bang the gavel. I want you to come with us.

MRS. JACOBY   Listen—Jerry's father I like very much, but Jerry's mother and me— Is there a law that says the bride and groom's family have to love each other?

ALICE   Mama, I'm asking you. Please. Jerry has to tell his family about the new assignment, and we want you to be with us.

MRS. JACOBY   So when do *I* hear about the new assignment?

ALICE   Will you come?

MRS. JACOBY   All right, so I'll go to the vault in the morning and get my bar pin.
   (ALICE *laughs and hugs her as* JERRY *enters from the bedroom*)

JERRY   Now I'm ready for that drink.

ALICE   Jerry, Mama's busting to hear the news.

MRS. JACOBY   (*Eagerly*)   So already tell me. You got a new position? Where is it? In Washington, maybe?
   (*She and* ALICE *sit on the sofa.* JERRY *sits on the arm of the sofa and puts ice and Scotch in his glass*)

JERRY   Mama, finally I'm out of the consular service and into an embassy as Junior Economics Officer.

MRS. JACOBY   What embassy?

ALICE   (*Parrying this*)   And he's been raised from Class Five to Class Four.

15

MRS. JACOBY It's better if the numbers go lower?

ALICE It means that he starts at nine thousand and ninety-five dollars a year and goes up to ten thousand, six hundred and thirty in three years.

MRS. JACOBY That's already real money. But *where?*

JERRY Mama, I don't know whether you know how these promotions are made—

MRS. JACOBY So tell me!

JERRY Well, the determination of merit is made by the staff corps review panel of the State Department. They go over your whole service record, and you don't have a choice. They put you where they need you.

ALICE (*Taking the ball*) Jerry did such a wonderful job in Johannesburg and Marseilles, and the two of us knocked them dead in Costa Rica—

MR. JACOBY So where do you go now?

JERRY Well, after evaluating my performance records, they decided on this big jump. They sprung it on me yesterday, and Alice and I really celebrated.

MRS. JACOBY (*Almost bursting*) So let me celebrate too!

ALICE Mama, Jerry is going to be attached to our embassy in Japan.

JERRY It's a great opportunity, Mama. I'm to be on Mr. Noah Putnam's staff. He's the man who's going to conduct major trade negotiations with the Kishi government.

ALICE And Jerry's going to have a month's briefing in Washington with Mr. Putnam before we sail.

MRS. JACOBY (*Quietly*) And that means you'll be stationed in Tokyo.

ALICE That's it, Mama.

MRS. JACOBY And you'll be living with the people who killed your brother.

JERRY Mama, I know how difficult it is for you and how deeply you feel, but it's sixteen years ago. The world has changed. We're in the space age. Former enemies have become very important friends. We're just not going to have any world left at all if we keep on hating.

MRS. JACOBY Maybe you can go to a school and take lessons. Don't hate the Japanese any more—they're our friends. Don't hate the Germans any more—they're our friends. I don't know where to go to get such lessons. For me it's still like yesterday afternoon. (*Rising and moving to the kitchen door*) You're young, Jerry. You can still learn.
(*She goes into the kitchen*)

ALICE   Jerry, what are we going to do?

JERRY   Darling, believe me, Mama isn't any problem. She's a
very well-adjusted woman. She's fairly happy and she certainly tries to keep busy. She'll understand.

ALICE   That's not what I'm worried about. We're going to be
gone for three years. It's just that I hate to leave her here—
away from the only people in the world she really loves.

JERRY   Are you still thinking seriously about taking her with
us? Is that what you're trying to say?

ALICE   Yes, darling, I am. The government will pay her fare.
I looked it up in the regulations.

JERRY   Oh, darling, that's the least of it. What about *her,* Alice?
You're talking about a woman who's lived practically all her
life in Brooklyn and, let's face it, a very ingrown parochial
life. How do you transplant her to a foreign country—
        (ALICE *goes to him*)

ALICE   Oh, Jerry . . .

JERRY   Not just *any* foreign country—but Japan.

ALICE   She'll be so excited about going on a trip—traveling—

JERRY   The novelty will wear off in a month. What does she
do for the rest of the three years?

ALICE (*Putting her arms around him*) Look, Jerry—Tokyo is halfway around the world. Now—suppose I became pregnant. Wouldn't it be wonderful to have her around? Wouldn't it?

JERRY (*His arms about her*) I think it would be wonderful if you were pregnant, darling. I don't think having your mother around is going to accomplish that.

ALICE Well, I do know one thing it will accomplish. It will make me happy.
(*They separate as* MRS. JACOBY *enters from the kitchen*)

MRS. JACOBY We'll eat in about fifteen minutes. I forgot to put the light under the carrots and peas. (*She hesitates*) Jerry, I didn't act so nice before. I didn't say "hurrah" about your new assignment. So I went into the kitchen and I hollered at myself. I apologize.

JERRY There's no need for that, Mama.

ALICE You never have to apologize to us, Mama.

MRS. JACOBY Jerry's right. We *are* living in a new age with space ships and rockets and missiles. I don't have to like it, but it's here and so am I. I have to learn to live with it. It seems like everything's changed—everything except one thing—(*With a loving smile, she extends her arms*) The way I love you. So eat something, darling. So take a little finger food.

(*She and* ALICE *sit on sofa.* ALICE *picks up her glass of soda and offers a sip to* MRS. JACOBY. *Meantime,* JERRY, *standing, has been deeply moved*)

JERRY   Mama, how would you like to go with us?

MRS. JACOBY   I told Alice I'll go to your folks'.

JERRY   Mama, I don't mean to my folks'. I mean to Tokyo—Japan.

MRS. JACOBY   (*Rising—stunned*)   Alice—this is a joke or something?
        (ALICE *shakes her head*)

JERRY   No, It isn't a joke. It's all spelled out in the regulations. They take care of your fare and everything. Alice wants you to come and so do I.

MRS. JACOBY   Japan? How could I live in Japan?

JERRY   You and Alice could go sightseeing together. You could go shopping. You could do a million things, Ma.

ALICE   And we'd be together and it would take such a load off my mind.

MRS. JACOBY   And what would I like better, Alice? (*She strokes* ALICE's *face*) I appreciate it, and I thank you, but I don't think so. (*She crosses to kitchen door*) No, I don't think so. (*She turns and comes back one step*) How far is it to Japan?
        (ALICE *and* JERRY *exchange a joyous look*)

JERRY   About nine thousand miles.

MRS. JACOBY   Oi!
  (*She exits into kitchen*)

ALICE   Oh, Jerry.
  (*They embrace*)

Curtain

The scene: The deck of the S.S. General Wood. *A morning in July. Up center are three deck chairs with green cushions. Two similar chairs are angled at stage right. There is an exit down left. Just above this is a door marked "Sports Deck." When open, stairs leading upward can be seen. Down right is a door to the lounge. Just above the door are the lounge windows backed by Venetian blinds. Up right the deck continues above and beyond the lounge. The ship's rail and the sky can be seen at this section.*

At rise: It is a miserable gray day. MRS. JACOBY *is huddled in the middle chair, wearing a blue coat and hat and covered with a green ship's blanket. She has her purse. Her arms are folded and her eyes closed. A magazine lies on top of the blanket at her feet. She looks miserable and reacts accordingly when a whistle shrills over the ship's amplifier and is followed by:*

VOICE Now hear this: Lifeboat drill will be held at three o'clock this afternoon at boat stations designated in the staterooms. Please take your places wearing your life preservers. We promise not to keep you very long, but we want all of you to be sure to participate. Signing off.

Ina Balin, Gertrude Berg, and Michael Tolan,
as ALICE BLACK, MRS. JACOBY, and JERRY BLACK

(*As the ship's foghorn sounds,* MR. KOICHI ASANO *appears on deck upper right. He is a Japanese in his sixties, dressed in a navy blue raincoat and a white panama hat, and carrying an attaché case. As the foghorn sounds,* MRS. JACOBY *turns her head in the direction from which it comes and opens her eyes. She sees* MR. ASANO. *He lifts his hat politely but she coldly turns away. As he passes her, she opens her eyes and watches him with dislike and distrust. He exits down left as* ALICE *enters from the sports deck door. She is wearing a lovely yellow coat and carries* MRS. JACOBY'S *sewing bag*)

ALICE (*Crossing to* MRS. JACOBY) The air make you feel better, Ma?

MRS. JACOBY I'm all right.

ALICE (*Sitting on chair next to* MRS. JACOBY) Still squeamish?

MRS. JACOBY I'm fine.

ALICE Did you take the Dramamine?

MRS. JACOBY I don't like it.

ALICE They did you a lot of good on the plane.

MRS. JACOBY On the plane, I was like a piece of stone all the way.

23

ALICE I remember my first flight, Mama. I was scared to death, but you get used to it.

MRS. JACOBY Maybe someday I'll get used to seeing clouds upside down.
(*The foghorn sounds*)

ALICE I brought your sewing bag.
(*She hands it to her*)

MRS. JACOBY (*Taking it without interest and placing it on the floor*) If I feel better, I'll sew tomorrow.

ALICE Mama, you haven't eaten anything.

MRS. JACOBY At four o'clock they bring around hot tea and Hydrox and a little bought cake. I'll take some.

ALICE That's not enough, darling. Rabbi Brodsky told you when it's a question of health you've a right to eat anything.

MRS. JACOBY Since when is it a question of health?

ALICE It certainly is a question of health if you're going to starve yourself.

MRS. JACOBY I could lose a few pounds. It wouldn't hurt me. See what you got yourself into—bringing your mama along?

ALICE You've got to admit it's better than sitting alone in Brooklyn and me worrying about you.

MRS. JACOBY Why do you think I came? So you shouldn't worry. So what happens? You sit around all day worrying.

ALICE (*Smiles*) I won't if you'll just be yourself and talk to people. I hardly recognize you without a smile.

JERRY (*Entering briskly and cheerily from up right. He wears a light-colored raincoat and a blue scarf*) Hi, girls!
(*Kisses* ALICE)

ALICE Hello, darling.

JERRY (*Sitting on a deck chair*) Seen any dolphins yet, Ma?

MRS. JACOBY All I see is gray water.

JERRY Well, there'll be dolphins pretty soon—and flying fish and lots of other steamers.
(*The foghorn sounds as a lovely blond passenger enters left*)

LADY PASSENGER (*To each in turn*) Good morning! Good morning! Good morning!
(*They acknowledge her greeting as she crosses and exits right*)

MRS. JACOBY (*With first spark of interest*) She's a natural blonde, Alice?
(ALICE *and* JERRY *laugh. There is a pause as they try to think of ways to rescue* MRS. JACOBY *from her gloom*)

JERRY There's a movie tonight.

MRS. JACOBY (*Interested*) Which one?

JERRY *The Law and Jake Wade.*

MRS. JACOBY (*Turning away her head*) I saw that four months ago at the Albee. Robert Taylor's in it. (*Turning back to* ALICE *with a new thought*) You know, Alice, I think Robert Taylor is Jewish.

    (ALICE *and* JERRY *laugh*)

JERRY Mama, why don't you come on the upper deck with Alice and me while we play some shuffleboard? (*Enthusiastically*) As a matter of fact, why don't *you* get in the game. (*She demurs with a gesture and a weak smile*) No, Mama, you'd be great at it. All you have to do is hit a round piece of wood with a long stick.

MRS. JACOBY (*Smiling wanly*) All of a sudden I'm a Mickey Mantle.

    (*They laugh.* MR. ASANO *enters, carrying his attaché case*)

JERRY Good morning, Mr. Asano.

MR. ASANO (*Removing his hat*) Good morning, Mr. Black.

JERRY I would like you to meet my family.

MR. ASANO It would be an honor.

JERRY My wife, Alice—and my mother-in-law, Mrs. Jacoby.
(MR. ASANO *bows to* ALICE)

ALICE How do you do, Mr. Asano.
(MR. ASANO *then bows to* MRS. JACOBY)

MRS. JACOBY (*Coldly*) How do you do.

JERRY Both the ladies are going to Japan for the first time. As
a matter of fact, so am I.

MR. ASANO I should be very happy to be of any help. If perhaps
you wish to play golf at my country club or to make inquiries
of any kind, my office is completely at your disposal.

JERRY We're very grateful, but I hope we won't have to bother
you. I'm sure the Embassy will take care of everything.

MR. ASANO You have a most efficient embassy. Now, I beg to be
excused.
(*He bows, puts on his hat and crosses to settle himself
in a deck chair, placing his attaché case on the chair to his
right, opening it and busying himself with papers inside*)

JERRY Mama, sure you don't want to come and watch shuffleboard?

MRS. JACOBY I'm sure, darling. You go up. Alice needs the
exercise.

ALICE No, I'll stay here with you.

MRS. JACOBY Please. I'll feel better if you go. Please go. Jerry, take her.

(JERRY *takes* ALICE's *arm and they reluctantly leave, exiting to the sports deck.* MRS. JACOBY *adjusts the position of her feet, causing the magazine to fall to the deck. Before she can extricate herself from the blanket,* MR. ASANO *rises and comes over*)

Bob

MR. ASANO Permit me.

(*He picks up the magazine and hands it to her. She takes it without looking at him*)

MRS. JACOBY Thank you very much.

MR. ASANO You're welcome.

(*He tips his hat and returns to his work. She rises, holding the magazine in her hands, and starts to fold her blanket. There is the piercing sound of a ship's whistle. She jumps, looking in the direction of the sound and dropping the magazine*)

MR. ASANO (*Removing his hat and coming to retrieve the magazine*) That's simply the ship's whistle indicating high noon, Mrs. Jacoby. Nothing to be alarmed about.

MRS. JACOBY (*Taking the magazine, still not looking at him*) Thank you.

(*She returns to folding her blanket*)

MR. ASANO   The sea is extremely choppy this morning, but that is not unexpected at this northern latitude.
> (*Again the magazine falls and, again, he picks it up and hands it to her*)

MRS. JACOBY   Thank you very much.

MR. ASANO   May I inquire—have I done something to give offense?

MRS. JACOBY (*Gathering up her belongings*)   No.

MR. ASANO   If so, I should like to apologize humbly.

MRS. JACOBY   Not necessary.
> (*She starts off*)

MR. ASANO (*Flatly, moving toward her*)   You take this attitude because I am Japanese?

MRS. JACOBY (*Stopping and turning*)   Yes.

MR. ASANO   Because of the war?

MRS. JACOBY   Because of my son.
> (*She again starts off*)

MR. ASANO   He was in some way affected? (*She stops but does not answer*) I wish you would tell me, please.

29

MRS. JACOBY (*Turning*) All right. (*She crosses back to him*) It was all in a telegram: "The Secretary of War has asked me to express with deep regret that your son, David Elias Jacoby, was wounded in action in Attu, on May 14, 1943. Address mail to Sergeant David Elias Jacoby, 147329, care of Hospital Directory Section, A.P.O. San Francisco." Signed— Ulio, Adjutant General. Then they sent for us. By the time we could get to our child he was gone. Yes, Mr. Japanese, my son was in some way affected.

(*She starts to go*)

MR. ASANO Our son was killed on a destroyer of the Thunder class by an American dive bomber. (*She stops and turns*) Our daughter was a nurse at Hiroshima in August, 1945, when your Air Force paid a visit. She, fortunately, did not survive.

MRS. JACOBY All because you and Mr. Hitler wanted to run the world.

MR. ASANO My wife and I did not so wish, Mrs. Jacoby. Nor our son, nor our daughter—nor anybody we knew. All we wished for was a happy and peaceful existence with the flowers, the moon, and the sunshine. Is that very different from what you wished, Mrs. Jacoby?

MRS. JACOBY (*Softly, sadly*) No.

MR. ASANO Then shall we start again? (*He moves one step closer, bows*) How do you do.

30

MRS. JACOBY   How do you do.

(*As they stand looking at each other, the foghorn sounds,
and the lights dim*)

Curtain

SCENE 3

The scene: The deck of the S.S. General Wood. *The next
morning.*

At rise: The atmosphere is light and sunny. JERRY *is sitting
in the far left deck chair, reading a book.* MR. ASANO *enters from
down left, dressed in a dark suit, no hat, and carrying his attaché case.*

MR. ASANO   Good morning, Mr. Black.
   (*He crosses to his chair*)

JERRY   Good morning, Mr. Asano.

MR. ASANO   How is your wife?

JERRY   Fine, thank you. She's playing shuffleboard on the upper deck.

MR. ASANO (*Sitting, placing the attaché case on the chair to his
   right*)   I wish I had the energy. I hope your mother-in-law
   is feeling better this beautiful morning.

JERRY (*Sitting up*)   Yes, sir, she is.

MR. ASANO   I regret if I perhaps upset her yesterday.

JERRY   She told me about it. I think she does understand a little now. It's very difficult for her.

MR. ASANO   She has every justification. Many people in my country hate the Americans unreasonably because of the war. I sometimes wonder which is worse—war or its aftermath of hatred.
   (*He opens his attaché case*)

JERRY   I think, sir, in the case of our two countries, we have made rapid strides towards understanding.

MR. ASANO   To some degree, yes. But there are still massive problems.
   (*He takes papers from case*)

JERRY   No problem is unsolvable for men of good will.

MR. ASANO   Do you realize, sir, we both sound as though we were making after-dinner speeches? (*He smiles ironically*) You will be a distinct addition to your Embassy.
   (*He returns to his work*)

JERRY   (*Trying not to show irritation*)   I plan to try, sir.

MR. ASANO   (*Turning from his work*)   Do you also plan to acquaint yourself with the problem of free markets—a subject that generates more heat than good will?

JERRY   The entire matter is under intensive study, sir.

33

MR. ASANO For the meeting in August? (JERRY *turns, surprised.* MR. ASANO *rises, removing glasses and crossing to him*) No, Mr. Black, I have not been reading your mail. My own government has asked me to participate. You might, if you will, call me Mr. Putnam's opposite number. It is, perhaps, fortunate that we have met under these agreeable circumstances and can discuss these matters on a less formal level. If you would care to see some figures from the Japanese point of view, on the textile question—I have with me—

JERRY (*Interrupting*) No, sir, I do not. You agree, Mr. Asano, that by August the situation may have leveled off, and we'll both be better prepared to make considered evaluations of your figures.

MR. ASANO (*Sharply*) No, sir. I do not agree. However, I understand that you obviously have been well-briefed and do not wish to become involved in an indelicate debate.
(JERRY *stands, uncomfortable.* MRS. JACOBY *enters from the deck, carrying her bulging sewing bag*)

MRS. JACOBY Good morning, Jerry.

JERRY Good morning, Mama.

MR. ASANO Good morning, Mrs. Jacoby.

MRS. JACOBY (*Making the effort*) Good morning, Mr. Asano. (*Suddenly he begins to cough. She looks at him, worried, then dives deep into her sewing bag and comes up with a small box. She offers it to him*) I have some Smith Brothers cough drops. Good for coughing.

MR. ASANO (*Takes box, extracts one and puts it in his mouth*) Thank you.

MRS. JACOBY   Jerry, I have Life Savers if you want one.

JERRY   No, thanks, Ma.

MR. ASANO (*Extending box to* MRS. JACOBY) Excellent flavor. And very soothing.

MRS. JACOBY   Keep them. I have plenty.

MR. ASANO   Thank you very much.
   (*He puts the box in his pocket. There is the shrill blast of the boat's whistle*)

MRS. JACOBY (*Smiling*) I know. It's twelve o'clock, high noon. (*Looking at her watch*) My watch says one, because I forgot to put it back the hour last night.

MR. ASANO   Try to remember that next Wednesday we cross the international date line and lose an entire day.

MRS. JACOBY   How do I do this on my watch?

MR. ASANO   Do nothing. It's Tuesday. Then it is Thursday.

MRS. JACOBY What happens to Wednesday?

MR. ASANO You get two Wednesdays on the way back.

MRS. JACOBY For me, that won't be for a long time.
(*She sits in a deck chair*)

MR. ASANO Time will pass quickly. There will be so much to see and to do.

MRS. JACOBY (*Hopefully*) There will?

MR. ASANO Oh, yes. Tokyo is a very modern city, Mrs. Jacoby. Not like those Japanese prints—all small pine trees and quaint curved bridges. We pride ourselves we're quite cosmopolitan.

MRS. JACOBY (*She has taken out her sewing*) Japan has a lot of people who aren't Japanese?

MR. ASANO Oh, yes. Many Westerners. (*Sitting to her right, trying to help*) I have been thinking. There's a most attractive Jewish Community Center behind the Red Cross Building.
(JERRY *looks up from his book, surprised and puzzled*)

MRS. JACOBY (*Warmly*) That's very nice of you to tell me.

MR. ASANO I imagine this is your first trip abroad?

MRS. JACOBY No. My third.

MR. ASANO Usually to Europe?

MRS. JACOBY I *started* in Europe. I was born in Kovno—that's Russia.

MR. ASANO I was in the Soviet Union last summer.

MRS. JACOBY In my day, it was plain Russia—with a Czar. That's why my father escaped to New Haven to my uncle, so he shouldn't have to serve in the Czar's army. Then a year later, my sister Gussie—then my sister Rachel—then my mother, and in 1912 I was elected. That was some long trip! First I had to cross the border in a hay cart so the Cossacks shouldn't see me. Then I went to Scotland. Finally, I got on a boat—but not to North America. South America—Argentina. And would you believe it? I couldn't speak a word of English. That's how I got on the wrong boat. (MR. ASANO *and* JERRY *listen attentively*) So I worked on a sewing machine in Argentina for a year and a half. My father finally sent money and, to make a long story short, I finally got to Castle Garden, a greenhorn. So that's how this is my third trip abroad.

MR. ASANO May I ask, Mrs. Jacoby, how old were you when all this happened?

MRS. JACOBY Who carries around a birth certificate? But, like my mother used to figure it out, I was born the fifth candle of *Chanukah,* in the year after mother's father died. When I finally got to New Haven, I was—a month pro or con— twelve and a half.

MR. ASANO You were a very, very little girl to have had all that trouble.

JERRY Mama, I never heard that story.

MRS. JACOBY Listen, I nearly forgot myself, until I smelled the ocean. Then all of a sudden, it came back to me—*precipitado!*

MR. ASANO You remember your Spanish?

MRS. JACOBY When I was little, I spoke it very good. I've met so many foreigners I've picked up a little Polish, a little Russian, a little Hungarian, a little Hebrew—Yiddish, I knew—and what I still remember of Spanish is *si, si, señor.* (MR. ASANO *sneezes*) You're sitting in a draft?

MR. ASANO No. I had a little cold when I got on board. I don't think I'm over it yet.
(*She dives into the deep recesses of her sewing bag and comes up with a bottle of aspirin*)

MRS. JACOBY Oh, yeah, so here, take a little Bayer aspirin.

MR. ASANO Thank you, but I took an antihistamine this morning.

MRS. JACOBY (*Disapproving*) See? Now, that I don't like! I wouldn't do that unless it was absolutely necessary. You're dizzy?

MR. ASANO Perhaps a little.

MRS. JACOBY To me the best medicines are always the simple ones: soap and water and stewed prunes. (*This is too much for* JERRY *who rises, smiling and shaking his head*) Where you going, Jerry?

JERRY I'm just stretching, Mama.
  (*The deck steward enters and hands the ship's news-papers to* MR. ASANO, MRS. JACOBY *and* JERRY, *and exits.* MR. ASANO *puts his in his pocket;* MRS. JACOBY *stores hers in the sewing bag, and* JERRY *studies his for a moment before folding it and putting it in his pocket.* MR. ASANO *sneezes*)

MRS. JACOBY (*Taking folded blanket from the back of her chair and giving it to him*) Here. Take a blanket. When you have a cold you should keep your feet warm.

MR. ASANO (*Covering his legs and feet with it*) Thank you. My wife shared your respect for warm feet, Mrs. Jacoby.

MRS. JACOBY She's—?

MR. ASANO She died two years ago last May.

MRS. JACOBY So you had a cupful, too. (*Remembering*) I lost my husband also—not quite four years ago. (*A slight pause*) She was sick long?

MR. ASANO From the time they made the diagnosis until the end—three very short—long weeks.

MRS. JACOBY My Sam was sick almost fifteen months. Would you believe that up to the last minute he was active in business?

MR. ASANO What was his business, Mrs. Jacoby?

MRS. JACOBY Artificial flowers.
    (JERRY *sits and starts reading his book*)

MR. ASANO I have a small subsidiary that makes artificial flowers.

MRS. JACOBY You have? (JERRY *looks at her, worried*) If you'll excuse me, the Japanese were our worst competitors.
    (*Alarmed,* JERRY *closes the book sharply. She glances at him, unconscious of any problem*)

MR. ASANO Your flowers were much better. Ours were made at cheap production costs to meet a special market. Mostly Woolworth's.

MRS. JACOBY (*Proudly*) We sold to Nieman Marcus, Bullock's, Filene's in Boston—

MR. ASANO Your husband must have had a very fine business.

MRS. JACOBY We were comfortable. Of course, everything went during his sickness. (*Sadly*) I miss the business.

MR. ASANO You were active?

MRS. JACOBY I kept the books, and believe me, Jacoby and Company paid their bills by the tenth and always took the discount.

MR. ASANO That is a most efficient way of doing business.

MRS. JACOBY Look who's talking to *you* about business. (*Patting* JERRY's *arm*) My son-in-law tells me you're a very important man.

MR. ASANO (*To* JERRY, *who leans forward, uncomfortable and uncertain*) I am delighted to hear your son-in-law has such a high opinion of me.
(*He bows and* JERRY *bows in return*)

MRS. JACOBY Tell me—what else do you do besides making artificial flowers?
(JERRY *is worried*)

MR. ASANO We have cotton mills, Mrs. Jacoby. We make velveteens, fabrics. The trouble is, Mrs. Jacoby, I no longer have any enthusiasm for trading in the market place. I should retire.

MRS. JACOBY I imagine you have a few dollars. You wouldn't starve.

MR. ASANO However, to me, retirement is a bleak prospect.

MRS. JACOBY   I understand. You have to be doing things. Life has to have salt.

MR. ASANO   Yes, Mrs. Jacoby, life has to have salt.
(*He sneezes again*)

MRS. JACOBY   (*Putting her sewing in the bag and preparing to rise*)   You want to take my advice—go into your cabin and take a cup of tea with lemon and honey and every half-hour gargle with hot water and peroxide. (*She rises. The men rise*) You got peroxide?

MR. ASANO   No, but I'm sure I'll be all right.

MRS. JACOBY   All I have to do is look at your eyes and know you have a temperature.
(*She starts delving again into her sewing bag.* MR. ASANO *watches, amused*)

MR. ASANO   What other miracles do you have deep in that bag, Mrs. Jacoby?

MRS. JACOBY   I had a thermometer, but I must have left it in my valise. I'll go get it. You want something, Jerry?

JERRY   No, thanks, Mama.

MR. ASANO   I do not like to put you to all that trouble.

MRS. JACOBY   (*Crossing to lounge door*)   It's no trouble. And on the way, I'll stop and talk to the dining room steward. (*Turning at door*) From *me,* he expects anything. You know, Jerry, the way he looks at me, I'm sure he thinks I'm *meshugeh.*

(*She exits laughing.* MR. ASANO, *puzzled, closes his attaché case, then turns to* JERRY)

MR. ASANO   What does "my-sugah" mean, Mr. Black?

JERRY   My mother-in-law uses that word so often she forgets it isn't English. It means crazy—(MR. ASANO *looks at him sharply*)—well, not insane but, let us say, scatterbrained.

MR. ASANO (*Crossing to* JERRY, *attaché case in hand*)   Well, Mr. Black, if your mother-in-law is "my-sugah," it is clearly a very delightful thing to be.

(*As they bow and start to move off, the lights dim*)

Curtain

*The scene: The same. An evening a week later. The two
deck chairs at right have been removed.*

*At rise: The deck is dimly lit by moonlight. Music is playing
over the ship's amplifying system.* ALICE *is standing at the rail
in a beautiful red and black gown. A young couple in evening
attire is standing stage left. They cross and exit. The steward
enters carrying a cablegram. He crosses and exits into the
lounge. A second couple enters and crosses to exit left.*

At this point, JERRY *enters from the lounge, wearing a dinner
jacket and carrying* ALICE's *stole. The music stops.*

JERRY (*Placing the stole about* ALICE's *shoulders*) Here you
are, darling.

ALICE (*Looking out front*) Thank you, sweetheart. I saw lights
out there.

JERRY (*Arms about her— both facing front*) Probably the fish-
ing fleets.

ALICE I thought it might be land.

JERRY Not till tomorrow night. Are you anxious?

ALICE Frankly, I'm a little scared. Aren't you?

JERRY Well—apprehensive. It's another new country—another new job—another new set of problems.

ALICE And protocol and etiquette and all those wives I have to call on.

JERRY You'll handle it. (*They kiss. Four bells is sounded*) That's four bells or—to us landlubbers—(*He looks at his watch*)—ten o'clock.

ALICE Mama go to her cabin?

JERRY (*Coming back to her*) No, she's having a brandy with those people from Djakarta. When I passed she was saying something about a spring form.

ALICE (*Laughing*) That's the pan for her famous economy lemon icebox cake.
  (*She crosses to sit in the center deck chair*)

JERRY (*Following*) Oh, yes. The one with the five million calories.

ALICE It worked out all right, didn't it, Jerry?

JERRY What?

45

ALICE   I was so afraid at first but, thank goodness, she's come out of her depression.

JERRY   That she has! She treats the entire passenger list as though they were her nephews, or nieces, or cousins.

ALICE   When I see her with Mr. Asano—gossiping away as though he were an old friend on a park bench—

JERRY   About *that,* I have reservations.

ALICE   You do?

JERRY   Well, tonight he sent another bottle of champagne to the table. I don't like to get gifts from people with whom I have to do business.

ALICE   I'm sure no congressional investigation committee's going to accuse you of conflict of interest over two bottles of wine.

JERRY   I think Mr. Asano plays with different rules.
        (*He sits in a deck chair*)

ALICE   He's just a lonely old man with a bad cold, and any cold that gets near Mama is a fool. My father used to say that everyone cried on Mama's shoulder. Even people on trains—when we went to the country—within half an hour they'd be telling her the story of their lives and asking for advice.

JERRY Hasn't anybody ever taken advantage of her?

ALICE Jerry, if Mr. Asano is trying to get around Mama, she'd be the first one to know it—believe me. (*Rising*) She has built-in radar.

JERRY (*Rising and following*) Darling, I have radar, too. Built out of some pretty dreary experience.

ALICE Jerry, I know what you're worried about, but I've been pleading with Mama to get out and mix with people. Now that she has, I can't ask her to stop.

JERRY I don't mind her mixing with people, but she doesn't have to adopt them. Over and over in the briefings, Mr. Putnam warned that, in the foreign service, you never know where a chain reaction's going to begin. You've got to anticipate trouble. You've got to try to stop it before it starts. (MRS. JACOBY *enters from the lounge. She is wearing a beautiful black gown and a lovely blue scarf. She's obviously happy and alert*) I'm only telling you—I anticipate trouble.

MRS. JACOBY Enjoying the sea breeze, darlings?

ALICE Yes. I hear *you've* been sipping brandy.

MRS. JACOBY You told me to be sociable. They're very nice people. He's the doctor with Standard Oil, and they live in a compound with ten *amahs,* which is how you say servants in Indonesia.

47

ALICE (*Touching her scarf*)   Mama, I never noticed this scarf before. Very French.

MRS. JACOBY   Mr. Asano gave it to me. He bought it for his daughter-in-law, but he wanted me to have it as a remembrance for the cough drops. It's a very Japanese custom called *Okaeshi*.

(JERRY *looks glum, turns away*)

ALICE (*Covering*)   It's lovely. That was very sweet of him.

MRS. JACOBY   I like it.

ALICE (*Crossing to* JERRY)   Jerry and I are going to play bridge, Mama.

MRS. JACOBY   I know—with the English people. You know, she's American. She met him in Los Angeles when he was a vice-consul.

JERRY   There's not a biography on this boat you don't know, Mama. Do you tell everybody about us?

MRS. JACOBY   When you're proud of your children, you talk about them.

ALICE   Want to come watch us play?

MRS. JACOBY   No, I'm meeting Mr. Asano. We're going to play dominos. You know, I won a dollar from him. He'd be a very good player if he'd concentrate. He talks too much.

JERRY (*Trying to be light, but probing*) What does he talk about, Ma?

MRS. JACOBY You know what a man talks about—business. He's got a lot on his mind.

JERRY Like what?

MRS. JACOBY Like duty.

ALICE Duty?

MRS. JACOBY On his goods. Jerry understands what I'm talking about. There's going to be a big conference in August.

JERRY Yes, I know that, Mama.

MRS. JACOBY Believe me, he's depending on you, Jerry. He respects you. He's a good man for you to know—and don't think I didn't tell him all about your degrees.
  (*She moves to the boat rail.* MR. ASANO *enters carrying a board and box of dominos. He bows*)

MR. ASANO Good evening, Mr. and Mrs. Black. (*They acknowledge his greeting*) I've just had a radio from my office in Tokyo. They're sending a car and a station wagon to meet me at Yokohama. If your Embassy has not made arrangements, please feel free—

49

JERRY (*Interrupting*) All arrangements have been made. Thank you, sir.

MR. ASANO   I thought we might play out here, Mrs. Jacoby. It's quite stuffy below decks.

MRS. JACOBY   Fine.

MR. ASANO (*To* ALICE *and* JERRY)   Perhaps you would care to join us? Four-handed dominos is very stimulating and quite unpredictable.

JERRY   Thank you, sir, but we do have a date.
(*The men bow.* ALICE *crosses below* JERRY)

ALICE   Please excuse us? See you later, Mama.
(JERRY *follows her*)

MRS. JACOBY   Go—make a slam. (*They exit into the lounge.* MRS. JACOBY *looks off into the night*) It's lovely out here in the night air. The moon is like a regular pumpkin tonight.

MR. ASANO (*Places the box and board on the center chair and joins her*)   In my country moon-viewing is traditional. We have a holiday for it.

MRS. JACOBY   A special holiday for looking at the moon?

MR. ASANO   It's called *Tsukimi*. Moon-viewing is held on the evening of the thirteenth day of September, comparable to the one held on the evening of the fifteenth day of August. If one participates in moon-viewing on the earlier occasion and fails to do so at this time, it is said to be "one-sided moon-viewing" and is not approved of. (*Taking her elbow to escort her back to the chair*) You think that strange, Mrs. Jacoby?

MRS. JACOBY No. In our religion we celebrate two days practically everything.

MR. ASANO Do you have many festivals?

MRS. JACOBY Oh, yes.
(*She sits on the chair*)

MR. ASANO In Japan we have a festival for almost everything. In spring it is called *Shun Bun No-Hi*.
(*He sits in a chair and arranges dominos on the board on a chair between them*)

MRS. JACOBY We have the same. In the spring, it's *Shevuoth*.

MR. ASANO In the fall, it's *Shu Bun No-Hi*. I hope you will celebrate *Shu Bun No-Hi* with me in the fall. We decorate our houses with grains and the fruits of the earth.

MRS. JACOBY We do the same. We have a *Sukeh,* a little hut we build, and put on grapes and apples.

MR. ASANO It sounds enchanting. I hope you will invite me to one of your festivals.

MRS. JACOBY   If we have a festival in Tokyo, you'll be invited, I assure you. But my children, I don't think they observe. You know how modern children are, Mr. Asano.

MR. ASANO   I know exactly how modern children are, Mrs. Jacoby.

MRS. JACOBY   But we have to learn to live modern, too.

MR. ASANO   That is difficult.

MRS. JACOBY   So what's easy? Whatever comes in your life, you take.

MR. ASANO   You transcend.

MRS. JACOBY   I beg your pardon?

MR. ASANO   You transcend. It is, in essence, the philosophy of the Zen Buddhists. To oversimplify what we believe: The torments of life are trials, successfully overcome, to achieve the serenity of the enlightened spirit.

MRS. JACOBY   You mean if a person has *tsurris*—trouble—you come out a better person if you live through it.

MR. ASANO   You have obviously studied Zen Buddhism.

MRS. JACOBY   (*Waltz music comes softly over the speaker*)   No.

I'm a plain woman. I've had my share of happiness, of worry, of *kwelling* from my husband and children.

MR. ASANO *Kwelling?*

MRS. JACOBY (*Smiling*) How can I explain *kwelling?* Well, *kwelling* is the way you look and the way you feel when something wonderful happens to somebody you love. It's—well, it's like when Alice graduated from Smith with the highest honors. It's pride—no, it's more—it's—it's *kwelling!*

MR. ASANO *Kwelling* would be an excellent addition to the Zen Buddhist vocabulary.

MRS. JACOBY (*Smiling*) If I should tell anybody I'm on a ship's deck, a thousand miles from Yokohama, explaining *kwelling* to a Japanese gentleman, who would believe it?

MR. ASANO *I* would be equally hard-pressed to explain it to my daughter-in-law.

MRS. JACOBY (*Smiling, she listens to the music*) I love that music. Sam and I took the children to that play on our anniversary. Afterwards, we all went dancing at the Copa. Sam always liked—(*Rising*) Whatever I do and whatever I say, I always come back to Sam.

MR. ASANO (*Rising and stepping toward her*) Would you care to dance, Mrs. Jacoby?

MRS. JACOBY I haven't danced in a blue moon.

MR. ASANO Nor I. Let us try.

MRS. JACOBY I couldn't.

MR. ASANO It is your idea. Live modern!
  (*They waltz, pleasantly and with dignity*)

MRS. JACOBY I didn't know they danced like this in Japanese.

MR. ASANO I learned to waltz at Oxford in 1919.
  (ALICE *comes in through the door and stands watching*)

MRS. JACOBY (*Happily*) Look, Alice! We're dancing!

ALICE I saw you through the window. I'm dummy, so I thought
I'd come out and join you.
  (*As the music ends, they stop dancing.* MRS. JACOBY *fans
  herself*)

Lani

MRS. JACOBY You get so warm when you dance.

Dob

MR. ASANO May I get you a cool drink, Mrs. Jacoby?

MRS. JACOBY I don't like to trouble you, but maybe a little
White Rock, please?

MR. ASANO (*Bows; he crosses to* ALICE) Can I get you something, Mrs. Black?

54

ALICE   No, thank you, Mr. Asano.

(He bows and goes into the lounge. MRS. JACOBY *looks closely at* ALICE*)*

MRS. JACOBY   What's the matter, Alice? You have a look on your face like when you used to cut school.

ALICE   *(Taking her elbow and guiding her to the chairs)* Mama, come and sit down.

MRS. JACOBY   What's the matter, Alice? What happened all of a sudden?

(They both sit)

ALICE   Look, Mama, when I first went to Costa Rica with Jerry, I met a woman, a Costa Rican, the wife of a cabinet member. She was wonderful to me. I really depended on her. And then one day she came to me and asked me to ask Jerry to talk to the Prime Minister because her husband was being fired. And I realized what a babe in the woods I was. I was just being used.

MRS. JACOBY   So. You think Mr. Asano is just being nice to me because of Jerry?

ALICE   In a month, Jerry will be in an important hassle with Japanese manufacturers—of whom Mr. Asano is the most important. Am I making myself clear?

MRS. JACOBY   I understand plain English.

55

ALICE Our government is trying to get the Japanese to voluntarily cut down exports—before Congress passes a restrictive tariff act. You know what a restrictive tariff act is, Mama?

MRS. JACOBY Yes. Your papa and me wrote to our congressman for such an act before you were born.

ALICE I'm sorry, Mama. I keep forgetting you were in business.

MRS. JACOBY And in business, with one look you know what a person is, and I tell you, Mr. Asano is an honorable man. (*She rises*) And he's not being nice to me so Jerry should be on his side.

ALICE (*Rises and crosses to her*) Try to understand, darling. In the foreign service, you have to be careful of easy friendships. Now, I was so glad you found somebody to talk to but, on the other hand, you must admit it was a little odd. After all, he is a—(*She cannot bring herself to say "Japanese"*)—a millionaire.

MRS. JACOBY Oh, and there's a law that says Mrs. Jacoby can only talk to paupers?

ALICE No, certainly not. The only point is—he *is* a Japanese.

MRS. JACOBY And I think he's from Texas.

ALICE Mama, please think about what I'm saying.

MRS. JACOBY   I am thinking, Alice. I'm thinking how you told me to mix and mingle and be like everybody else. So I stick one toe in the water and already I'm drowning. All right— so go back to your bridge game. And don't eat your heart out. If that's what you want and if that's what Jerry wants, I won't talk any more to that—that *goniff!*

ALICE   Mama, you didn't have to say that.

MRS. JACOBY   That's what *you* were trying to say.

ALICE   No, Mama—
   (*She stops as* MR. ASANO *enters from the lounge, carrying a glass of White Rock which he gives to* MRS. JACOBY)

MRS. JACOBY   Thank you.

MR. ASANO   What about our game, Mrs. Jacoby?

MRS. JACOBY   I was just talking to Alice and tomorrow is our last day out and I have so much packing to do—I thought I'd go to my cabin and get my packing in motion.

MR. ASANO   I understand.

MRS. JACOBY   Mr. Asano, I want to thank you for the scarf—for the dancing—for everything.

MR. ASANO   It has been my pleasure. Now, I beg to be excused.
   (*He bows and exits into the lounge*)

ALICE Mama, you handled that like a diplomat.

MRS. JACOBY Some diplomat! Thank you for the compliment. (*She hands* ALICE *the glass*) I thought I was making a friend out of an enemy. So what did I do? I made an enemy out of a friend.

(*She crosses to exit*)

Curtain

ACT TWO

SCENE I

The scene: Two months later in the living room of the BLACK *home in Tokyo. It is late on a rainy Thursday afternoon.*

It is a rented, Western-style house, decorated in ugly browns and greens. Up center is an ugly Chinese breakfront on which are a TV set and a small radio. It is flanked by two straight chairs. At right is a sofa. Far right is the bookcase which doubles as a bar. A small round table and two chairs are at left. A window is at left and, below it, an arm chair. Up left are double doors leading to the outside door, kitchen and rest of house. Up right is the door to ALICE *and* JERRY'S *bedroom.*

At rise: MRS. JACOBY *is just finishing ironing one of* JERRY'S *shirts at a board set up just above table left. She looks at her watch and goes to turn on TV. The reception is dreadful. Disgusted, she turns it off.*

MRS. JACOBY *(Calling)* Eddie!

EDDIE *(Off)* Yes, madame.
> *(She returns to the ironing board and puts the shirt on a hanger as* EDDIE *comes in. He is a grinning young Japanese houseboy, wearing black trousers and vest and a gray coat. He carries a dish towel)*

61

MRS. JACOBY Eddie, take away the ironing board, but first fix the television. The up and down doesn't stop and, when it does, it's like herringbone tweed.

EDDIE I will tune it properly.
(*She disappears into the bedroom as he hangs the towel over his shoulder, turns down the lights and tunes in the set. A Japanese Elvis Presley appears, emitting a Japanese version of rock 'n' roll.* EDDIE *delightedly snaps his fingers to the music until* MRS. JACOBY *re-enters. He grins and waits expectantly for her reaction*)

MRS. JACOBY (*Returns and peers at the picture*) Elvis Presley I can get in Brooklyn.

EDDIE Oh, but we are hepcats for American music.

MRS. JACOBY Please get my channel. There's a love story on every day at this time.

EDDIE But that is in Japanese, Jacoby-san. How you understand it?

MRS. JACOBY By the pictures. The couple are always arguing because she's jealous, so I figures out he has another woman.

EDDIE Oh, no! It is *she* who has another man.

MRS. JACOBY When I look at it my way, it's "John's Other Wife." So get it, Eddie.
(EDDIE *turns the dial, and Sumo wrestlers go at it full blast. He is very excited*)

MRS. JACOBY   So where's my program?

EDDIE   It has apparently been replaced by the championship Sumo wrestling. Shall we watch them?

MRS. JACOBY   Eddie, please—

EDDIE   You don't like Sumo wrestling?

MRS. JACOBY   What's to like? They sit around and squat and then they jump up like crazy people and give each other such a smash.

EDDIE   (*Pointing*)   This one number one smasher. I have bet on him.

MRS. JACOBY   Good luck. Turn it off and put on the lights. (EDDIE *turns off the TV and turns on the lights.* MRS. JACOBY *speaks hopefully*) Maybe something's on the radio. (EDDIE *turns on the radio. True Japanese music comes forth.* EDDIE *grins broadly, waiting for her reaction. She listens for an unhappy moment*) Try the armed forces station maybe.
   (EDDIE *changes the station. When there is no sound, he slaps the top of the set smartly*)

ANNOUNCER'S VOICE   In spite of the Chinese wall that's helped the home-run average of the local boys, the Los Angeles Dodgers must love that cellar because last night they had a chance to get out of it and they blew it when the San Francisco Giants massacred them again, twelve to four, with Willie Mays getting four for four—

63

MRS. JACOBY (*Disgusted*) Turn it off, Eddie.

EDDIE (*Snapping it off*) Ah! It is terrible about the Los Angeles Dodgers.
  (*He unplugs the iron*)

MRS. JACOBY I don't want to hear about them since they moved from Brooklyn. (*She takes a magazine from the bookcase*) Now what'll I do?

EDDIE Why don't you go for a walk?

MRS. JACOBY In the rain?

EDDIE It stops and starts. You go between.
  (*He gestures with his hand—like a fish swimming upstream*)

MRS. JACOBY If I walk away one block from this house, I get lost.

EDDIE Why don't you go to the movies? I saw very good picture—*The Law and Jake Wade*.

MRS. JACOBY Again with Jake Wade.

EDDIE I like Robert Taylor. You know, Jacoby-san, I think Robert Taylor Japanese.

MRS. JACOBY (*She laughs, then leafs through the magazine*) I can't get used to American magazines without ads. (*She puts it behind her on the sofa with a sigh*)

EDDIE You will humbly pardon me. I must go attend to my duties.

MRS. JACOBY Where are you running to, Eddie? Sit a minute. Tell me about your girl. It's serious?

EDDIE She is of very old-fashioned family, Jacoby-san. We met through a *nakodo*.

MRS. JACOBY What's a *nakodo*?

EDDIE *Nakodo* is a relative or friend who arranges a suitable marriage.

MRS. JACOBY Ohh—a *shadchan*—a marriage broker.

EDDIE (*Shaking his head*) A *nakodo*. He has suggested we marry, but our families must study the suggested bride or groom as to heritage, health, interests, character—

MRS. JACOBY That's a very good idea.

EDDIE Ohh—not good. They do not like me because—(*Smiling at pleasant thoughts*)—I spend too much time in Shinjuku, which they consider to be very bad section of Tokyo.

MRS. JACOBY Is it?

EDDIE (*His smile broadens as he leans back importantly*) Ohhhh, it is very jazzy there and I am well respected. (*Confidentially*) You know, Jacoby-san, if you were to get a few cartons of cigarettes and some whiskey and some French perfume from the Embassy commissary, I could sell them on the black market and we could split the profit!

MRS. JACOBY Eddie, don't be such a business man and don't make me your partner. (*She rises. He rises*) And, Eddie, don't ever let me hear such talk in this house again! Never again let me hear it!

EDDIE Oh, I go work for the Canadian Embassy!

MRS. JACOBY No, Eddie. Please! Canadian Embassy! Eddie, I don't want my daughter upset.

EDDIE If you were to part with a few miserable yen, I might consider—

MRS. JACOBY Again, yen! (*Sound of outside door slamming*) No more, Eddie!
  (*At that moment,* ALICE *enters wearing a raincoat over a cocktail dress. She is just removing her head scarf*)

ALICE Why were you ironing in the living room, Eddie?

EDDIE (*Smiling slyly*)   I was not ironing, Black-san. Jacoby-san was ironing.

ALICE   Oh, I see. Hello, Mama-san.

MRS. JACOBY   Hello, Alice-san.
(*As they hug,* MRS. JACOBY *shakes her finger at* EDDIE. *His grin broadens*)

ALICE   Were there any messages, Mama?

MRS. JACOBY   Eddie takes the messages.

ALICE   Eddie?

EDDIE   Yes, Black-san. Your husband called and he asked me to give you the following message. He is now in conference with number one man.
(ALICE *and* MRS. JACOBY *exchange a happy look*)

ALICE   Thank you, Eddie. Anything else?

EDDIE   Only that Jacoby-san spoke to me without dignity. But I swallow my pride and stay for few more miserable yen each week.

ALICE   All right, Eddie. I'll talk to Mr. Black.
(EDDIE *bows and leaves*)

ALICE   It sounds like you had a run-in with Eddie-san.

MRS. JACOBY That Eddie-san is some bum-san.

ALICE You know how difficult it is to get servants who speak English. At least he takes messages. Number one man. That can only mean—

MRS. JACOBY Mr. Asano. Who else? It certainly is peculiar that he waited so long to go to Jerry's big meetings at the Embassy. On the boat that's all he talked about.

ALICE It's a diplomatic technique, Mama. Play hard to get. Make everybody nervous. You heard Jerry explain it last night.

MRS. JACOBY Did you tell Jerry what I told you about my davenport?

ALICE I mentioned it, but—well, I think it's best for neither one of us to interfere, don't you? I mean, I'm sure Jerry's gone over every possible alternative.

MRS. JACOBY But, Alice, I've had a lot of practical experience and if Jerry would speak to that Mr. Putnam—

ALICE Mr. Putnam is a very difficult man, Mama, so please don't say anything to Jerry.

MRS. JACOBY All right. Did you have a nice time at the French Embassy today?

ALICE A wonderful time. And I'm really very disappointed that you didn't come with me.

MRS. JACOBY I went with you a couple of times to your high society. It didn't turn out so good. I was afraid to say something wrong.

ALICE Mama, you're too sensitive.

MRS. JACOBY (*Flatly, as she starts to deal solitaire*) With me, I try never to make the same mistake twice.

ALICE (*Brightly*) What did *you* do today, Mama?

MRS. JACOBY I watched television and, don't holler, I ironed Jerry's tuxedo shirt.

ALICE I wasn't going to mention that, Mama, but you really shouldn't have. Remember what I told you about losing face with the servants. (*Hugging her*) But they can't iron like you. Jerry's going to look wonderful at General Thurman's tonight. (*Lightly*) What are you going to wear? Your black dress with the bugle beads?

MRS. JACOBY I'm not going. If I can't talk to civilians, what would I say to a general?

ALICE Mama, please.
(*The outside door slams*)

MRS. JACOBY Don't push, Alice. I'm not going. Jerry?
(JERRY *enters wearing a raincoat and carrying his attaché case. He's tired*)

ALICE Hello, darling.

JERRY Hello. Hello, Mama.

ALICE Conference go okay?

JERRY Could have gone better. I saw Mr. Asano today. He says hello.

MRS. JACOBY I'm glad he's so friendly.

JERRY I wouldn't exactly say that. Alice, may I have a drink?

ALICE Sure. Would you like one, Mama?

MRS. JACOBY (*Rising*) No, I'm not so hotsy totsy with drinking. I'll go get the ice.
(*She exits*)

JERRY I'll take it without ice, Alice.
(*He sits on the sofa*)

ALICE (*She pours Scotch and water from the pitcher into a glass*) Darling, you look exhausted.

JERRY I'll tell you why I look exhausted—because I am.

ALICE You must have had a hard day.

JERRY It was a beaut.

ALICE (*Handing him the drink and sitting*) Tell you what—
why don't you take a nice hot bath and I'll scrub your back
like any good Japanese wife and you can tell me all about it.

JERRY Let me have the drink first.

ALICE I made you a double. Why don't you finish the drink
and then take a nap. And I'll serve you dinner in bed. We
don't really have to go to General Thurman's tonight.

JERRY Yes, we do.

ALICE Nobody'll miss us. It's going to be a very big party.

JERRY Yes. Big and dreary and a *must!*

ALICE All right. You should have seen me today. I went to
the French Embassy and there were about forty women—
all in Dior originals. They served champagne in the drawing
room and jasmine tea in the conservatory—
      (*The phone rings.* JERRY *goes to answer it*)

JERRY That sounds very classy, honey. (*Into phone*) Hello
. . . Yes, this is Mr. Black . . . Hello, Mr. Putnam . . . Yes
. . . I see . . . Yes, I did feel it was particularly directed
against me . . . No, sir, I can't assign a reason . . . When

71

do we resume? . . . I see . . . Yes, sir, I'll prepare my notes and report to you tomorrow morning at nine thirty . . . All right. Good-bye, sir. (*As he hangs up the phone*) Alice, I have to have a talk with your mother.

ALICE (*Surprised*)   A talk with my *mother?*

JERRY   Yes—with your mother.

ALICE   I don't know if my *mother* is available. Would you like to talk to Mama?

JERRY   All right, I can do without the sarcasm.

ALICE   Jerry, what's the matter with you? What's Mama got to do with it?

JERRY   I don't know. What did you tell your mother on the boat about Mr. Asano?

ALICE   Exactly what I told you.

JERRY   Did she ever talk to him again after that night?

ALICE   How do I know?

JERRY   Well, don't you think we ought to find out?

ALICE   Jerry, before you put Mama on the carpet, there are a few things *I've* got to find out—

JERRY The conference was a disaster.

ALICE Why?

JERRY Guess!

ALICE Obviously I'm too stupid!

JERRY You couldn't be that stupid! Didn't I tell you on the
boat—
  (*She stops him as* MRS. JACOBY *enters with a bucket of
  ice*)

ALICE Thank you, Mama. Jerry, I think we'd better get dressed
soon.

JERRY We have some time. I want to look over some things.
  (*He gets his attaché case, sits on the sofa, opens it and
  starts to look at papers*)

ALICE Mama, would you like to play some cards?
  (EDDIE *enters*)

EDDIE Black-san, have you discussed my raise with your husband?

ALICE Not now, Eddie, please—

EDDIE In the meantime, I turn on television to see how Sumo
wrestling come out.
  (*He goes to the set*)

ALICE No, Eddie—

JERRY No, Eddie, you cannot turn on television to see how Sumo wrestling came out.

EDDIE Jacoby-san let me look at Sumo wrestling.

JERRY Well, I am not Jacoby-san. I am Black-san.

EDDIE I will not work in house where I am not allowed to see Sumo wrestling and where Mama-san gets the ice and irons the shirts and I am not allowed to have a few more miserable yen. I shall accept the offer of the Canadian *chargé d'affaires*.
  (JERRY *rises*)

JERRY Eddie—just a minute. Look—I'm sorry. We will be out of here in a few minutes and you can look at television to your heart's content. And we'll talk privately about your raise.
  (*He moves back to the sofa*)

EDDIE I am not respected.

JERRY (*Controlling himself with difficulty*) It is an honor to have you work here, Eddie.
  (*He bows deeply*)

EDDIE Thank you, Black-san.
  (*He bows and goes off with a triumphant grin at the women*)

74

JERRY   Now what's this about a raise?

ALICE   Well, you know how he is—

MRS. JACOBY   I said something to him, Jerry. That's why he's so mad.

JERRY   If you wouldn't interfere with Eddie, Mama, I think we'd all be better off.

ALICE   She doesn't interfere, Jerry!

MRS. JACOBY   Alice, please. Jerry is right. It wouldn't happen again.

JERRY   Mama, there's something I have to ask you.

ALICE   Do you have to ask her now, Jerry?

MRS. JACOBY   Just because Eddie said—something.

JERRY   It isn't about Eddie, Mama. It's about Mr. Asano.

MRS. JACOBY   Yes, you said he wasn't exactly friendly.

JERRY   No, Mama. He was, I might say, extremely cold.

MRS. JACOBY   Why?

JERRY   I don't know why, Mama. I'm trying to find out. What happened on the boat between you and Mr. Asano?

75

MRS. JACOBY You know what happened. We played dominos
—and we talked.

JERRY What did you talk about?

ALICE Mama, apparently Jerry had a very bad day at the conference.

JERRY Due mostly to your old friend, Mr. Asano, Mama. He
refused to accept our proposals or any compromise. So the
whole negotiation shattered into a million pieces—and we
start all over again. What do I mean *we?* Somebody starts
all over again, but without Jerry Black!

ALICE You were only one of five men at the conference. It's
not your fault.

JERRY Isn't it? Well, if you were there, you might not be saying that. Because our Mr. Asano took a personal delight in
needling me, and frustrating me, and making it perfectly
clear that he couldn't stand having me in the same room! Oh,
he bowed and I bowed and then we almost hit our heads
bowing—(*He bows deeply*)—but he took no pains to hide
his contempt for me. Everybody noticed it and they hurried
off like little bees to tell everybody else. It'll be better than
dessert at General Thurman's tonight, believe me.

MRS. JACOBY Why should he do that to you?

JERRY I don't know, Mama! Maybe you know the answer to
that better than I do.

ALICE Jerry, stop it!

MRS. JACOBY Maybe he didn't like my suggestions on the kind of fabrics he should make?

JERRY I did not discuss your suggestions on the kind of fabrics he should make. I just want to find out what you said to him —after Alice warned you.

ALICE I didn't *warn* her, Jerry!

MRS. JACOBY Whatever I was told to do, I did.

JERRY What did you actually say? You talked to him again, didn't you?

MRS. JACOBY Yes. When the boat landed he gave me his card and said I should call him if I wanted to go for a little sightseeing.

JERRY And what did you say after that?

MRS. JACOBY I didn't take it down in shorthand!

JERRY Was he angry?

MRS. JACOBY No, Jerry. He was polite.

JERRY Look, Mama—did you ever say to him that Alice and I didn't want you to see him because he was a Jap?

ALICE Jerry!

MRS. JACOBY (*Suddenly very angry*) What do you think I am?
A crazy old woman ready for a home for the aged? I'm not
a person? I haven't got a brain? What am I? A *shlemiel?*
An idiot?

ALICE Mama, it's all right.

MRS. JACOBY What's all right? It's all right I should sit in this
house afraid to open my mouth? That's all right? Well, it's
not all right! I'm a grown-up person and it's *not* all right.
And I want to go home!

JERRY Mama, we'll talk about your going home some other
time.

MRS. JACOBY We'll talk now! I got a few dollars in the bank—
enough to take me back to New York and bring me back to
Tokyo and take me back to New York again. So for *me* you
don't have to worry!

ALICE Mama, I don't want you to go and that money's your
savings.

MRS. JACOBY My savings for a rainy day?! And today the sun
is shining! I am going home and I want no more cross-
examinations!

ALICE Jerry, talk to her!

78

JERRY   Your mother's a grown woman, Alice. If she wants to go home, she knows what she's doing.
(*He picks up the attaché case*)

ALICE   Is that all you have to say? Well, then I'm going with her!!

JERRY   Oh, Alice, let's be reasonable.

ALICE   Reasonable about what? Jerry! I just wanted to find out something. You come home hurt and wounded about some rotten little conference. You shout and raise your voice. You act as though we were both your enemies!

JERRY   (*Shouting*)   All right!!
(*He goes into the bedroom, leaving the door open*)

ALICE   I am fed up! You are just like your mother!

MRS. JACOBY   (*Quietly*)   Maybe he thinks you're like *your* mother—(ALICE *crosses and places her hands on* MRS. JACOBY's *shoulders*)—always in the wrong place at the wrong time. It's not your fault. It's not Jerry's fault. It just happened. Go in and talk to him. You'll say "A" and he'll say "B" and you'll get glad. Go. (ALICE *reluctantly goes into the bedroom, closing the door.* MRS. JACOBY *begins to cry miserably. After a moment, she goes to her purse on the end of the sofa, sits, takes a handkerchief from it and dries her tears. As she replaces the handkerchief, she sees and takes out* MR. ASANO's *card. She studies it a moment and then quickly crosses to the door up left. She calls softly*) Eddie.

EDDIE Yes, madame.
(EDDIE *enters*)

MRS. JACOBY Eddie, how far is this from here?
(*He takes the card, reads it and is impressed*)

EDDIE Asano-san! It is in the district Den-en-cho-fu. Half-hour by automobile.

MRS. JACOBY So call me a taxi.

EDDIE I cannot phone for a taxi. I will have to go out on the street and get one.

MRS. JACOBY So I'll go with you. And, Eddie, promise me you wouldn't tell anyone where I'm going.

EDDIE I promise.

MRS. JACOBY And write me down on a piece of paper—write me the address—where it is, and the telephone number—in Japanese. (*He writes*) Are you sure you're writing it right?

EDDIE Oh yes—Jacoby-san.
(*He finishes and tears off that slip*)

MRS. JACOBY And on another piece of paper write where *this* house is and *this* number.
(*He writes and gives her a second slip*)

EDDIE Jacoby-san, you don't know where you live?

MRS. JACOBY   Oh, I know where *I* live—776 Eastern Parkway,
Brooklyn, the United States, *North* America!
  (*She exits*)

Curtain

SCENE 2

The scene: MR. ASANO'S *living room, a half-hour later.*

It is a lovely Japanese room. The right portion is screened off to form a vestibule. There are shelves in the wall on which are a statue of Buddha and one or two objects of art. Left of the shelves is the Tokonoma. *Its central feature is a* kakemono, *a wall scroll. Just below the* kakemono *is a typical Japanese floral arrangement. Just left of the* Tokonoma *is the post symbolizing the center of the house. The left half of the back wall is formed by screens which are open, giving a beautiful view of the porch and the gardens beyond.*

At rise: MR. ASANO, *in* kimono *and wearing his glasses, is seated cross-legged on a* zabuton [*cushion*], *reading a book. His arm is cradled on an arm rest.* NOKETI, *a beautiful maid, kneels to his right, fanning him as he reads. As he turns a page, reading from right to left, there is the melodious tinkle of the doorbell. It is repeated as a* HOUSE BOY *enters, crosses quickly and silently on bare feet, opens the screen into the vestibule and goes up to slide open the outside door.* MRS. JACOBY *steps inside, wet and disheveled.*

Throughout the following, English translations of the Japanese appear in brackets.

MRS. JACOBY   Mr. Asano lives here, yes?

BOY (*He does not understand English*)   *Donata samadesuka?*
[May I have your name?]

MRS. JACOBY   *Mr. Asano?*

BOY   *Eigo ga wakarimasen.* [I cannot understand English.]

MRS. JACOBY   Somebody speaks English here, maybe?

BOY   *Su mi ma shen. Su mi ma shen.* [I am sorry. I am sorry.]

MRS. JACOBY   English?
(*At the first sound of her voice,* MR. ASANO *has laid aside
his book, removed his glasses and left them with the
book, risen and crossed to the vestibule. He is delighted
to see her*)

MR. ASANO   Mrs. Jacoby! what a surprise!
(BOY *closes outside screen*)

MRS. JACOBY   Please excuse me, but I have to talk to you.

MR. ASANO   But you are wet! How did such a thing happen?

MRS. JACOBY   I came in a taxi and I got out and he disappeared
—and I've been looking all over. There are no numbers.

MR. ASANO   Now it is *you* who will catch cold. Please do me
the honor to enter my house.

> (*As he extends his hand and she starts forward, the* BOY
> *protests, pointing to her shoes*)

BOY   *Choto kutsuo.* [Wait—the shoes!]

MR. ASANO   It is customary to remove your shoes.

MRS. JACOBY   Oh, I don't mind.

> (BOY *kneels and removes her shoes as* MR. ASANO *takes
> her hand to steady her*)

MR. ASANO   Will you come this way, and please excuse the disorder of my house.

> (*She follows him into the living room.* BOY *places the
> shoes against the vestibule wall and follows them, leaving
> the screen open.* MR. ASANO *goes to* NOKETI *and addresses
> her*)

MR. ASANO   *Heya o katazuke te, ayako ni sugukuru yoni
linasai.* [Please rearrange this room for an honored guest.
And ask my daughter-in-law to come in immediately.]

NOKETI   *Hi!* [Yes, sir!]

> (*She hurries out, bowing as she goes*)

MRS. JACOBY   I don't like to trouble you, but if I could just—

MR. ASANO   The entire facilities of my house are completely at your disposal. (MRS. AYAKO ASANO, *a beautiful Japanese woman in her late thirties, enters wearing an elaborate* kimono. *She kneels*) Mrs. Jacoby, this is my daughter-in-law, Mrs. Ayako Asano.

(MRS. JACOBY *extends her hand, but* MRS. AYAKO *is already bowing very deeply*)

MRS. AYAKO   *Irasshaimase. Yoku irrassahi mashita.*

(TATESHI, *a servant of the household, and a* MAID *enter, kneel and bow*)

MR. ASANO   She says, "Welcome! Oh, how good of you to come." (*To* MRS. AYAKO) *Kono kataga nay-ay-nee hanashta Jacoby fugin deh, funay no nakadeh o-eye-eeshta kahtadess. Anata no kimono-o kash-tay agenahsai.* [This is the lady I told you about that I met on the boat, Mrs. Jacoby. She is an extremely honored guest. Please see to it that she removes her wet clothing so that she will not catch cold, and provide her with other suitable garments—the best we have in the house.]

MRS. AYAKO   (*Rising*) *Do-zo kochira-ne.* [Please accompany me.]

MR. ASANO   My daughter-in-law says if you will accompany her, she will do her best to make you comfortable.

MRS. JACOBY Thank you very much. I hope I'm not disturbing your supper or something.

MR. ASANO It is an honor to have you in my house, Mrs. Jacoby. It is something for which I have wished for for a long time.

MRS. JACOBY Thank you.

(*He bows.* MRS. JACOBY *returns his bow. She turns and bows to* BOY, *who bows. She then bows to* TATESHI *and* MAID *who bow. She then follows* MRS. AYAKO *off*)

MR. ASANO (*To servants*) *Niku o tsukawanai yoo ni. Ichiban-yoi utsuwa o dashinasai.* [Please arrange to provide a suitable dinner for our guest of honor. You are to use a new set of dishes and we are to have no meat—only fish that comes from the lake. All food will be broiled and barbecued without any additional fats of any kind. And you may proceed with the ceremonial.]

MAIDS *Hi! Kashiko marimashita.* [Yes, sir, we understand.] (*The girls bow and leave.* BOY *kneels and moves the arm rest back against the wall, places* MR. ASANO's *book and glasses on a* zabuton, *and carries them out.* MR. ASANO *moves Buddha up from a lower shelf. He steps back to view his work and crosses down left.* BOY *enters with a low mahogany table which he places center and exits. Meantime,* TATESHI *enters with a short black* kimono *on a tray, and assists* MR. ASANO *in putting it on.*

During this, MAID *has entered with a blue cushion on top of a yellow one and places them left of table.* NOKETI, *immediately behind her, brings an orange cushion on top of a maroon one and places them above table.* MAID *and* NOKETI *exit.*

NOKETI *returns with one orange cushion which she places right of the table. She exits.* NOKETI *returns with a yellow rose in a vase.* MAID *follows her in with a tray of tea, service for three, and two cold, moist towels. She places the tray right of the table.* NOKETI *places the rose on a lower shelf and kneels at a corner of the table.* TATESHI *picks up the empty* kimono *tray and exits.* MAID *exits*)

MR. ASANO (*Looks over their preparations, then to* NOKETI) *Mo ichimai.* [One more *zabuton.*]
（*She bows, rises, and exits, returning immediately with another maroon* zabuton *which she places atop the two above table. She looks at* MR. ASANO, *then drops her head behind her sleeve to hide a smile.* MR. ASANO *indicates dismissal and she exits.*

MRS. JACOBY *hesitantly enters, after a moment, wearing a Japanese* kimono, *the* obi *high around her waist. She's embarrassed and shy*)

MRS. JACOBY Madame Butterfly.

MR. ASANO You look lovely, Mrs. Jacoby. Will you do me the honor to sit at my table. (MRS. AYAKO *enters and kneels by the table*) I am sorry we have no Western chairs, Mrs. Jacoby,

87

but I think you will find the *zabuton* not too uncomfortable.
(*Gingerly,* MRS. JACOBY *permits him to assist her in sitting on the three cushions*)

MRS. JACOBY   It's very comfortable. This is how you live? It's like a travelogue.

MR. ASANO   It is a great honor that you grace my house.

MRS. JACOBY   I want to talk to you about something very important—

(MRS. AYAKO *has placed the two towels, in their baskets, before them on the table, then the tea things. As he speaks,* MR. ASANO *picks up a towel and prepares to use it.* MRS. AYAKO *indicates to* MRS. JACOBY *that she should do likewise.* MRS. JACOBY *watches* MR. ASANO *closely and imitates his action*)

MR. ASANO (*Wipes his hands*)   In Japan, conversation is not apt to begin until after the formalities have been carried out. It is an aspect of Japanese etiquette often disconcerting to the uninitiated Westerner. I hope you do not mind. (*Tea is placed on the table, then he places his towel in the basket and pushes it away.* MRS. JACOBY *does exactly the same*) This is green tea. I trust you find it agreeable.

MRS. JACOBY   Tea is tea. (MRS. AYAKO *places a bowl of buns on the table.* MR. ASANO *sips his tea.* MRS. JACOBY *carefully imitates*) Lovely flavor. It tastes like—hot parsley.

(MRS. AYAKO *removes the towels.* MR. ASANO *picks up the buns*)

MR. ASANO These are bean-jam buns, served only when we have the honor of a visit from an important stranger.

(*He offers them. She takes one and samples it*)

MRS. JACOBY Delicious. It tastes like—Halvah.

MR. ASANO My daughter-in-law will see that you have some upon your departure.

(*He drinks*)

MRS. JACOBY Thank you. Beautiful china. It's so lovely on the tray.

(*She drinks*)

MR. ASANO (*To* MRS. AYAKO. *As he speaks,* NOKETI *enters and kneels*) *Omiyage-ni agenasai.* [Please see that Mrs. Jacoby is given an identical set of china.]

MRS. AYAKO *Hi!* [Yes, sir!]

MR. ASANO I have instructed my daughter-in-law that you be given an identical set.

MRS. JACOBY Ohh—thank you.

NOKETI *Tadaima omeshimono o kawakashite orimasu.* [We are drying and pressing the lady's clothes. They will soon be ready.]

MRS. AYAKO *Arigato Naru beku hayaku.* [Thank you. Do it as quickly as possible.]

(NOKETI *bows, rises and exits quickly*)

MR. ASANO I understand your garments are in the process of being restored. It will not be long.

MRS. JACOBY Thank you.

MRS. AYAKO *Otoh sama. Kono kimono yoku oniainianaru desho sashi agetara do desho?* [I hope the lady will accept the gift of the *kimono*. It is very becoming to her.]

MR. ASANO My daughter-in-law hopes you will do her the honor of keeping the *kimono* that you are wearing. She feels that it is most becoming to you.

MRS. JACOBY Thank you. It's beautiful, but I couldn't.

MR. ASANO Made the more beautiful by your wearing it, Mrs. Jacoby.

MRS. JACOBY Thank you. Mr. Asano, I want to talk to you about my son-in-law, Jerry—

MR. ASANO (*Rising, extending a helping hand*) Mrs. Jacoby, let me show you my house.

MRS. JACOBY (*Rising with some difficulty*) Oi!

90

MR. ASANO As you probably have observed, our room is very simply decorated. Unlike Westerners who fill their rooms with many beautiful things, we select only one or two. The floor is covered with *Tatami* mats because, to us, the floor is the place where we live and sleep and so we like to keep it sweet and clean. In the winter, we use sliding panels to make the room as warm as possible. In the hot summer months we remove them to bring in the summer evening breezes and the sounds of the night. (*He touches the post*) This post symbolizes the center of the house. (*Moving to the* Tokonoma *and indicating the whole area*) This is the *Tokonoma*—the place of honor as it has been since the days of the shoguns, the ruling lords of Japan.

MRS. JACOBY Very interesting. And what you do with flowers!

MR. ASANO My daughter-in-law will see that you have all the flowers—

MRS. JACOBY Please! It's enough already! Mr. Asano, I want to talk about my son-in-law, Jerry. You see—

MR. ASANO We have not yet finished our tea and cakes. (*He assists her to sit. He resumes his seat*) Mrs. Jacoby, I am forced to break my own custom because there is something on my mind.

MRS. JACOBY Yes? What?

MR. ASANO I confess I have been a little angry with you.

MRS. JACOBY Oh, I'm sorry.

MR. ASANO We had such a pleasant relationship on board. You made a dull crossing most enjoyable.

MRS. JACOBY I'm very flattered.

MR. ASANO And then, suddenly, you saw fit to reassume a distant attitude.

MRS. JACOBY That is not what I came to talk to you about.

MR. ASANO I had a feeling that perhaps your children were involved in this decision.

MRS. JACOBY I'm very close with my children.

MR. ASANO However, it is not the children who should instruct the parents; but the parents who should instruct the children.

MRS. JACOBY Not in America.
(During the following, the servants remove the tea and cake plates and bring on a tray with two sake *cups and two* sake *decanters)*

MR. ASANO You are wise and venerable, Mrs. Jacoby, and only the venerable have enough experience and maturity to understand matters of personal relationships.

MRS. JACOBY   Jerry also understands, Mr. Asano. And if I did something that makes you mad at Jerry, I beg you not to take it out in business.

MR. ASANO   When I greeted him today in the usual manner, he bowed too low.

MRS. JACOBY   That's because Jerry isn't used to bowing.
(MRS. AYAKO *places the* sake *cups before them*)

MR. ASANO   I should have preferred a Western handshake.

MRS. JACOBY   But, Mr. Asano, Jerry—

MR. ASANO   Now we serve *sake,* Mrs. Jacoby. (MRS. AYAKO *fills their cups*) Rice wine. It is served hot and you will find it excellent against the inclement weather. (*He lifts his cup*) *Kompai.*

MRS. JACOBY   (*Lifting her cup*) My family say—*L'chayim.* Mr. Asano—we were talking about my son-in-law.
(*They drink.* MRS. AYAKO *refills their cups. During the following, after each drink,* MRS. JACOBY *rests her hand holding the* sake *cup on her knees, never looking at it. Each time,* MRS. AYAKO *refills it*)

MR. ASANO   I assume you know the nature of my business with your government.

MRS. JACOBY   Yes. I understand it didn't go so good today, because you're being very stubborn.

(She drinks; MRS. AYAKO *refills her cup)*

MR. ASANO   Stubborn? No. Practical. If we reduced our exports, it would mean a loss of employment for my workers and a severe blow to the national economy.

MRS. JACOBY   But that isn't Jerry's fault. Promise me you wouldn't hold a grudge against Jerry!

MR. ASANO   My personal feelings are not pertinent, Mrs. Jacoby. The issue here is one of principle.

MRS. JACOBY   So—you'll give a little and you'll get a little.

(She drinks. MRS. AYAKO *fills her cup)*

MR. ASANO   My government is well aware that we must give a little. The question is how much. Originally, your government asked us to reduce our exports of velveteens by a million yards annually. They now ask that we reduce them two million yards annually.

MRS. JACOBY   And they didn't suggest how you'll take up the slack?

MR. ASANO   They only promised they will use their best efforts. That is a phrase employed frequently by your son-in-law. I regret their best efforts are not good enough.

(He drinks)

94

MRS. JACOBY You're right. You can't take best efforts to a bank.

(*She drinks;* MRS. AYAKO *refills her cup*)

MR. ASANO How true.

MRS. JACOBY I tried to tell that to Jerry, but my daughter don't like me to mix in.

MR. ASANO Mrs. Jacoby, if you have any opinions, by all means "mix in."

MRS. JACOBY Yeah? You mean it? (*She accepts the invitation and plunges in happily*) So listen to a story about my davenport.

MR. ASANO (*Puzzled*) What is a davenport, Mrs. Jacoby?

MRS. JACOBY You don't know what a davenport is? By day, it's a couch and, at night, you pull it out and it's a bed.

MR. ASANO Ingenious.

MRS. JACOBY Well, I have a davenport in my apartment— (*To* MRS. AYAKO)—which, by the way, I still have a lease on it for another year—on my apartment—Apartment 3A— (*Back to him*)—and it's a beautiful piece of furniture. Originally, Sam and I bought it from Callahan and Driscoll on Livingston Street because Mr. Driscoll and Sam both belonged to the Elks and Mr. Driscoll gave us a lovely price.

95

MR. ASANO How friendly.

MRS. JACOBY Oh, listen. In the thirties, Mr. Driscoll had plenty of trouble. Because he sold only the best Grand Rapids furniture, and who could afford it in the thirties? But he was a very smart man—he took in a budget line—budget carpets and budget carpet sweepers and he came over the depression.

MR. ASANO He diversified.

MRS. JACOBY Exactly—he diversified. And that's the first thing *you* should do.

MR. ASANO I agree, Mrs. Jacoby. But in what area? Our market studies so far have given us no indication.

MRS. JACOBY Market studies—(*Drinks*)—the best market study is personal experience. (*She drinks;* MRS. AYAKO *pours more sake, and for the first time* MRS. JACOBY *notices that her cup is being constantly refilled. She does a double take*) So where was I? (*She smooths her hair, trying to think*) So where was I?

MR. ASANO I believe you were with your davenport.

MRS. JACOBY (*Happily*) Oh, yes—my davenport. Last year, company came to the house. The Rosensweigs who live in 4B, and Essie Rubin who lives in 3H, and Essie brought along her Mr. Wechsler who's in the fountain pen game. Well, Mr. Wechsler took from his pocket his absolutely-guaranteed-against-leaking fountain pen—and what happened? (*She nods; he nods. She makes a sweeping gesture*) All over the davenport! So Essie and Mr. Wechsler nearly died. The next day, Mr. Wechsler came over with a special ink remover—(*To* MRS. AYAKO)—which he also manufactures. (*Back to* MR. ASANO) It worked. It removed the ink. It also removed the material.

MR. ASANO (*Amused*)   I feel very sorry for Mr. Wechsler.

MRS. JACOBY   I couldn't be sadder. But I had to have my davenport re-covered. (*To* MRS. AYAKO) So I decided on baby blue—(*She stops as she sees* MRS. AYAKO *does not understand*) Baby blue—baby—(*She rocks her arms as though cradling a baby*) A-a-a-a-a-a, baby. (*Then back to* MR. ASANO) So I had to run around to A & S, Macy's, Gimbel's. You know what you have to pay for upholstery material in America?

MR. ASANO   My market reports indicate a minimum of two dollars a yard.

MRS. JACOBY   *You* go find for two dollars a yard. (*To* MRS. AYAKO—*holding up five fingers*) Five dollars is more like it. (*Back to him*) So—maybe I came to it all around the mulberry bush—this is what I want to tell you. Here, in Japan, with cheaper production costs—you should concentrate on manufacturing inexpensive upholstery material and, you'll see, you'll have no competition in the United States.

(*She drinks.* MR. ASANO *rises*)

MR. ASANO   Thank you, Mrs. Jacoby. I will restudy the market research in that field.

(She sets the cup on the table, rises and crosses to him)

MRS. JACOBY   All you have to worry about is—can you modify your looms.

MR. ASANO   *(Smiling)*   You even know about that.

MRS. JACOBY   I'm also practical. *(Happily, nudging him with her elbow)* So—so it's settled?

MR. ASANO   I'm afraid not, Mrs. Jacoby. You see, I have a board of directors to deal with and stockholders—and my government's view as well.

MRS. JACOBY   So why did you let me talk?

MR. ASANO   You may not have brought a solution, but what you *have* done is to erect a signpost. You have forced me to probe more deeply—and I promise you—I will probe.

MRS. JACOBY   Good!

MR. ASANO   I had concluded that today was the final meeting. I have changed my mind. As a compliment to you, Mrs. Jacoby, I shall continue my discussion with your government.

MRS. JACOBY   With my government or with my son-in-law?

MR. ASANO With your son-in-law.

MRS. JACOBY (*Shaking his hand*) Thank you, Mr. Asano! Well, I've taken up enough of your time. I'll go and get a taxi.

MR. ASANO Oh, no, Mrs. Jacoby. You must stay for dinner.

MRS. JACOBY (*Frightened*) It's very kind of you, but I already had a very early dinner.

MR. ASANO I do not think that is so—

MRS. JACOBY Yes, yes.

MR. ASANO No. You are afraid to eat in my house. You have heard that we eat raw fish and octopus.

MRS. JACOBY (*Aghast, looking at* MRS. AYAKO *and back to him*) I never heard such a thing! Never!

MR. ASANO It is true. But I have ordered a special dinner for you to be served on a new set of china, consisting of dishes entirely compatible to—kosher!

MRS. JACOBY (*Laughing*) How do you know about kosher?

MR. ASANO You told me.

MRS. JACOBY I told you! On the boat!

MR. ASANO (*To* MRS. AYAKO) *Shokuji-o hakobinasai.* [Prepare to serve the meal.]

MRS. AYAKO *Hi!*
(She rises with the tray of sake *bottles and cups and goes out onto the porch, where she kneels, sets down the tray and closes the two outside screens, shutting out the view of the garden. She then exits with the tray)*

MRS. JACOBY (*As* MRS. AYAKO *is leaving room*) She's such a nice lady. I wish I could talk to her. She doesn't speak one word of English?

MR. ASANO None whatsoever. Of course, that is not very peculiar, Mrs. Jacoby, because you do not speak one word of Japanese.

MRS. JACOBY Who says? I can speak. (*She thinks*) I can say, for instance, please, which is *dozo.* And I can say thank you, which is *arigato.* And—wait—wait—(*Giggling*)—one more. You're welcome, which sounds like Don't touch my mustache!

MR. ASANO (*Laughing*) With those three phrases, you'll always be happy in Japan.

MRS. JACOBY (*Bowing*) *Arigato.*

MR. ASANO Don't touch my mustache. (*She turns away, giggling. He looks at her for a minute and then at the scroll, the* kakemono, *which hangs in the* Tokonoma) Mrs. Jacoby, there is one thing I have not explained. (*He points to the scroll*) Have you observed this scroll?

MRS. JACOBY It's very pretty. Is it hand painted?

MR. ASANO Yes. It is an old Japanese art. As you see, it shows an ancient emperor at one side of a bridge and a lady of the court at the other. The bridge symbolizes that tl.ey are apart. The question is—should they cross the bridge?

MRS. JACOBY Is there any reason they shouldn't?

MR. ASANO The emperor was a widower and there was much opposition to his remarriage.

MRS. JACOBY You don't say?

MR. ASANO Despite his treasures, he was lonely. And when he met this lady he was much drawn to her—even though she was of another province—not of royal blood and, indeed, of another religion. But after due consideration and the cutting off of a few heads—

MRS. JACOBY Ohh—that wasn't nice!

MR. ASANO Perhaps not. But, finally, all opposition silenced, he crossed the bridge to her—(*He moves slowly towards her. She is turned away*)—slowly and steadily, taking great care not to stumble.

MRS. JACOBY Good!

MR. ASANO   So you think the emperor was right?

MRS. JACOBY   If they loved each other, what business was it of anybody else?

MR. ASANO   They did not meet properly, of course, through a *nakodo*.

MRS. JACOBY   (*Nodding—pleased with her knowledge*)   A marriage broker.

MR. ASANO   They did not permit a proper lapse of time, as is our custom in arranging betrothals.

MRS. JACOBY   We also have such a custom. Sam and I kept company for two years.

MR. ASANO   As a consequence, they did not, for instance, go to plays, concerts and national events so that they could learn to know each other. Do you think that was wrong?

MRS. JACOBY   When you're old, there's not much time. I think the emperor was right.

MR. ASANO   I am not sure I agree with you.

MRS. JACOBY   Why don't you agree? What difference would it have made if they had gone to plays, concerts, and national events?

MR. ASANO   It is a question of etiquette.

MRS. JACOBY Sometimes you can carry etiquette too far.

MR. ASANO Nonetheless, I am old-fashioned, Mrs. Jacoby. I like to observe the proper form. (*He adjusts the neckline of his* kimono *and moves down to her. He bows*) Mrs. Jacoby— (*She turns to him*)—would you do *me* the honor of accompanying me throughout the winter to plays, concerts, and national events?

MRS. JACOBY (*Aghast as she grasps his meaning*) Mr. Asano!

MR. ASANO But, Mrs. Jacoby, I was sure that you understood my allegory. I was obliquely referring to both our persons.

MRS. JACOBY To me it was just a very interesting story.

MR. ASANO Mrs. Jacoby—given time—perhaps we, too, might cross the bridge and together achieve the serenity of the enlightened spirit. In the meantime, it can do us no harm to be friends.

MRS. JACOBY (*Shyly*) I would like very much to be friends.

MR. ASANO Then shall we have dinner? (*He extends his hand. She hesitates*) Dozo.
  (*She permits him to lead her to the table and they resume their seats. He claps his hands twice*)

MAID (*Off*) Hi!

MR. ASANO   You look most appropriate at the head of my table, Mrs. Jacoby.

MRS. JACOBY   Some appropriate.
> (MRS. AYAKO *enters and kneels at the table.* NOKETI *enters, carrying a tray of appetizers, and kneels to her right, pushing the tray in front of her.* NOKETI *remains in this position to assist in the serving.* TATESHI *enters and kneels at the table with a tray bearing fish and chopsticks. She places them on the table.* MAID *enters, bearing a large bowl of fruit, and kneels and places it to the left of* NOKETI, *who hands it to* MRS. AYAKO *who places it on the end of the table.* MAID *leaves.* BOY *enters with a tray bearing rice bowls and a large container of rice. He places the tray near* NOKETI *who spoons rice into the bowls and hands them to* MRS. AYAKO *to place on the table.* TATESHI *exits.* MAID *enters with* Koto *and places it to the left of the table.* TATESHI *enters with* Samisen *and kneels with it by the* Koto. TATESHI *and* MAID *begin to play and sing)*

MR. ASANO   Mrs. Jacoby, you are our most honorable guest.

MRS. JACOBY   Oh, Mr. Asano, all of a sudden to be a most honorable guest!
> (*They look at each other as* BOY *enters with a large bowl of raw vegetables and kneels. The girls sing*)

Curtain

ACT THREE

Scene 1

The scene: The living room of the BLACK *home. Later that evening.*

At rise: JERRY *is sitting in a chair by the table. His coat is on the back of his chair. On the table are an empty beer bottle and a half-eaten sandwich on a small plate. He drains the glass as* ALICE *enters from the bedroom.*

ALICE   Want anything else, Jerry?

JERRY   No, thanks.

ALICE   What time is it?

JERRY   (*Looking at his watch*)   Not quite eleven o'clock. The last show at most of the downtown movies is just about letting out, so we ought to be hearing from Mama pretty soon.

ALICE   Jerry, I don't think she went to the movies. Not alone on a rainy night.

   (*The sound of a car coming to a stop and the door slamming*)

JERRY (*Looking out the window*) That must be Captain Norcross.

ALICE Who's Captain Norcross?

JERRY He is an American attached to the Japanese police as interpreter. I called him about an hour ago—just routine.

ALICE You're really worried, too.

JERRY No, I'm not. It's just that Captain Norcross—
(*There's a buzz at the door. JERRY goes out to answer it*)

CAPTAIN (*Off*) Good evening, Mr. Black. I've been assigned to the Jacoby case.
(ALICE *reacts, turning quickly*)

JERRY (*Off*) It was very nice of you to come, Captain Norcross. Won't you come right in. (JERRY *enters, followed by the* CAPTAIN, *a young and sedate man in civilian clothes*) This is my wife. Darling, this is Captain Norcross.

CAPTAIN Delighted, Mrs. Black.

ALICE Why did you call it the Jacoby case?

CAPTAIN That's just a convenient identification, Mrs. Black. So far, we have very encouraging news. We've checked all the hospitals and all the jails in the area—and the morgue—all reports of automobile accidents and other violence and, as far as we can determine, as of the present moment, eliminating imponderables, of course, Mrs. Jacoby is not involved.

ALICE   Just what do you mean by imponderables, Captain?

CAPTAIN   Well, we haven't heard yet from the prefectures of the outlying districts.

ALICE   My mother is not in the habit of going to outlying districts.

CAPTAIN   We can never be sure, Mrs. Black. Just recently we had a case where an American woman was found with her throat—Well, enough of that— Now, let me see if I have the description straight. Your husband told us over the phone, Mrs. Black, that your mother is five foot two and a half.

ALICE   Five foot three.

CAPTAIN   In her early sixties?

ALICE   Fifty-eight.

CAPTAIN   Tell me, was she in any way mentally disturbed?

ALICE   Certainly not!

JERRY   Darling, she *was* a little upset.

ALICE   All right, Jerry—let's tell the Captain the truth. She was more than upset. We had a crisis here this evening.

JERRY   Oh, it wasn't really a crisis.

ALICE   Then just to the *brink* of one—

CAPTAIN   *Brink* is a word we don't like to use around here, Mrs. Black. Now tell me about your mother. Is she in the habit of going off on little jaunts like this all by herself?

ALICE   Of course not.

CAPTAIN   Has she been out in the city much? Sightseeing?

JERRY   Well, Captain, I doubt if she'd be sightseeing in weather like this.

CAPTAIN   That's true! Well, how long ago did she leave?

JERRY   It must have been about six o'clock. We went inside for a few minutes and when we came out she was gone.

ALICE   And so was the house boy, Eddie.

CAPTAIN   Yes, Mrs. Black, your husband told us that on the telephone. (*Consults his notebook*) His name is Iricho Watanabe. Number 1, 1-chome, Shinjuku, Tokyo, Japan.

ALICE   It seems to me the first thing you'd do would be to go and find him.

CAPTAIN   We have already been there, Mrs. Black. He wasn't

home. However, the Japanese authorities have posted a man. But I don't like that Shinjuku business.

ALICE Why not, Captain?

CAPTAIN Well, Shinjuku is—well, shall we say—a district where marginal characters are likely to resort.

ALICE Oh, my God!

CAPTAIN Please—please—let's not be alarmed. What we three must determine—after discounting violence or accident, is where would we go if we were an American-Jewish woman, fifty-eight years old, five foot three, at eleven o'clock on a rainy Thursday night in Tokyo. (ALICE *and* JERRY *watch as* CAPTAIN NORCROSS *thinks. He has one thought and discards it with a shake of his head. He thinks again, then shakes his head. After a third try—*) You know, I haven't the faintest idea.

> (*The sound of the outside door slamming.* JERRY *rushes out.* ALICE *stands just inside and below the door*)

JERRY (*Off*) Eddie, come in here a minute.
> (JERRY *enters, followed by* EDDIE, *who wears a Marlon Brando leather jacket*)

ALICE Eddie, where have you been? Where's my mother?

JERRY Now listen, Eddie. Have you seen Jacoby-san? Do you know where she went?

EDDIE   Oh, no, sir.

JERRY   I don't believe you, Eddie. I don't like that look in your eye.

CAPTAIN   Please, Mr. Black. Allow me to do the interrogation if you don't mind. I am Captain Norcross. I'm attached to the Metropolitan Police. I want you to answer some questions. Of course, I know you are not involved in any way.

EDDIE   Oh, no, sir.

CAPTAIN   Where have you been this evening?

EDDIE   To the movies.

CAPTAIN   What picture did you see?

EDDIE   *The Blob*.

CAPTAIN   Now then, Eddie, have you any idea where Mrs. Jacoby is?

EDDIE   I quit. I leave. I go to Canadian Embassy.
(*As he makes a move to go, the outside door slams again.* JERRY *dashes out and* ALICE *moves to just inside and below the door*)

JERRY   (*Off. So relieved he dares to be angry*)   Mama! Don't you ever dare leave this house again without telling us where you're going!

(JAPANESE CHAUFFEUR *in full livery enters, carrying packages wrapped in a cloth. He crosses and places them on the sofa. He is immediately followed by* MRS. JACOBY *and* JERRY)

ALICE   Mama! We're out of our minds.

MRS. JACOBY (*Lightly*)   I was visiting. (EDDIE *looks at the packages with curiosity. She opens her purse, takes out money and offers it to* CHAUFFEUR) *Arigato*, Jiro.
(*He holds up his hand in refusal, bows very low, and quickly leaves*)

CAPTAIN   Well, we're very relieved to see you here, Mrs. Jacoby.

MRS. JACOBY (*Very friendly—shakes his hand*)   How do you do.

JERRY   Mama, this is Captain Norcross. He was—well, he was looking for you.

MRS. JACOBY   I'm sorry you were worried, but time flies when you're enjoying yourself.

JERRY   Captain Norcross, we're very grateful for all your help.

CAPTAIN   I can see you won't be needing me any longer. Good night.

ALICE   Good night, and thank you very much.

CAPTAIN   Not at all. I'll see that headquarters gets the good news. And I'd suggest, Mr. Black, that you give General Thurman a ting-a-ling—and tell him that our lost little sheep has found her way home, wagging—(MRS. JACOBY *looks up sharply*) Uh—well—good night.
(*He exits hastily*)

EDDIE   You have received many lovely gifts, Jacoby-san.

MRS. JACOBY   *Arigato.*

EDDIE   (*Bowing*)   *Do-itashi-mashite.* [You're welcome.]

JERRY   That will be all, Eddie. I'm sorry, Eddie, if we disturbed you. We'll attend to everything in the morning.

EDDIE   It is an honor to work in a house where Mama-san comes home with a chauffeur and so many wonderful signs of the regard in which she is held. Good night.
(*He bows very formally and exits.* MRS. JACOBY *is softly singing the Japanese song while examining her bundle of packages. She does not look at* ALICE *and* JERRY *during the following.* ALICE *and* JERRY *watch her closely*)

JERRY   Mama, where have you been? Who was that chauffeur? What are all those packages?
(MRS. JACOBY *continues her singing*)

114

ALICE   Mama, did you have something to drink?

MRS. JACOBY   Aha. I had a few cups of hot *sake*.

JERRY   *Where,* Mama?

MRS. JACOBY   (*Placing her hat and gloves, which she has removed, on the table*)   Did you ever have *sake*? It tastes like hazel nuts. It's very pleasant.

ALICE   We were going crazy worrying about you.

MRS. JACOBY   Many times I went crazy worrying about you.
(*She sings, working at the knot of the bundle.* JERRY *gives* ALICE *a look*)

JERRY   (*Smiling*)   Mama, how much *sake* did you have?

MRS. JACOBY   I stopped counting.

ALICE   How long are you going to keep us in suspense? Where did you go?

MRS. JACOBY   I went to see Mr. Asano.

ALICE   Did he give you those gifts, Mama?

MRS. JACOBY   Yes. Did you ever see the way they wrap things? It's a shame to open them. In this package is bean-jam buns, pink and green. In this package is a *kimono* with an oh-boe—

(*She demonstrates an* obi) In this package is a set of china, service for two. And in this package is a flower holder so I should make Japanese flower arrangements.

ALICE   What were you doing there?

MRS. JACOBY   (*Happily*)   First we had tea and buns and then we had supper—a little milk soup with egg drops, then we had broiled fish—

ALICE   Mama, we're not interested in the menu.

MRS. JACOBY   If you want to hear the rest, you have to hear the menu. (ALICE *and* JERRY *are amused*) So we had broiled fish and, Alice, I could see there was nothing on it except a little butter. And we also had ginko nuts, called silver prunes, served on pine needles. And with supper his servant played on a long banjo. Jerry, I had a wonderful time! And then, after, Mr. Asano and his daughter-in-law and the servants took me out to the car—a car which the whole side goes up so I should get in.
   (*She illustrates*)

JERRY   That's a Mercedes Benz.

MRS. JACOBY   (*Great nonchalance*)   What then? Mr. Asano should have a Chevy? Jerry, maybe we have a little *sake* in the house?

ALICE   Why did you go see Mr. Asano, Mama?

MRS. JACOBY Well, I thought if I caused Jerry any trouble, I'd try to fix it up.

JERRY Well, I hope you didn't try, Mama.

MRS. JACOBY I did.

ALICE What did you say?

MRS. JACOBY Jerry, you can't blame Mr. Asano. Listen, first you ask him to reduce a million yards on velveteen. Then, all of a sudden, you ask him to reduce two million yards. Is that a way to do business?

JERRY Mama, you don't understand. We're having a lot of pressure put on us by the commerce department.

MRS. JACOBY Yes, but this is liable to cause Mr. Asano a very bad economic situation. However, if he can diversify he'll listen to reason.

JERRY Diversify?

MRS. JACOBY You already had such a discussion, no, Jerry?

JERRY In general terms—and he rejected it.

MRS. JACOBY Maybe now he wouldn't reject. I told him about my davenport.

JERRY   But, Mama. You can't just walk into Mr. Asano's house and talk about your davenport. This is a highly involved, technical—

MRS. JACOBY   What's so involved?
(*The phone rings.* JERRY *answers*)

JERRY   Hello . . . Yes, this is Mr. Black . . . Oh, hello, Mr. Putnam . . . Oh, I see . . . Yes. At ten o'clock . . . Yes, of course, I'll be there. Good night, sir.

ALICE   Well?

JERRY   (*Slowly hanging up the phone*)   There is a very important meeting tomorrow morning at ten o'clock with Mr. Asano and the Japanese representatives of the textile industries! (ALICE *and* JERRY *embrace happily, then stop suddenly and look at* MRS. JACOBY, *who gazes front with a slight pleased smile*) Mama, I guess *your* conference tonight was pretty successful. The government ought to put you on the payroll.

MRS. JACOBY   One high government official in the family is plenty. You know, Jerry, we really should have a little *sake* in the house.

ALICE (*Laughing*)   Tomorrow, I'll buy a case.

JERRY   Mama, I hereby present you with the first annual Jerry Black award for understanding and patience—

118

Arsenio Trinidad, Gertrude Berg, and Cedric Hard-
wicke, as HOUSE BOY, MRS. JACOBY, and MR. ASANO

MRS. JACOBY   Sha! One note of warning, Jerry. It's only the
beginning. Nothing is settled. Nothing is arranged. You're
just going to talk some more. Only, Jerry—
   (*She stops herself, patting her mouth with her palm, and
   sits in a chair*)

JERRY (*Kneeling*)   Go on, Ma. Have you got any more advice
for me?

MRS. JACOBY   I should give Jerry Black advice?

JERRY   You're holding back, Mama. Please don't.

MRS. JACOBY   I wouldn't sound like a mother-in-law they make
jokes about?

ALICE   Say whatever you want, Mama.

MRS. JACOBY   It's nothing important—only—well, you know one
of the reasons Mr. Asano got mad? Because you made a mistake, Jerry, and bowed too low—and he thought you were
making fun of his customs. I know you weren't making fun.
You just didn't know.

JERRY   I try to learn as much about Japanese customs as I can,
Mama, but I don't have much time.

MRS. JACOBY   And you don't have much time, Alice, either?
With the socializing and leaving calling cards and drinking
tea? But let me tell you something, children. It's very important how you speak to foreigners about the little things. I

know, because I was a foreigner for a long time and foreigners are very sensitive people. (*She hesitates*) And you don't have to overdo either. I mean, for instance, the way you treat Eddie. You don't bow to a boy like Eddie—not because he's a servant—and not because he's Japanese—but because he's *wrong*. It doesn't matter what color a person is—if he's wrong, he's wrong whether he's white, black, pink or purple.

JERRY Anything else on your mind, Mama?

MRS. JACOBY Yeah—

JERRY What?

MRS. JACOBY Jerry, when you talk to a business man, you have to *talk* not theories and best efforts, because best efforts you can't eat. You have to talk one—two—three. This—is—exactly —how—it—is. Or it's no sale.

JERRY (*Ruefully*) The State Department never explained it quite like that.

ALICE (*Hugging her*) Nobody ever had a mother like you in the world.

MRS. JACOBY Yeah—the whole world, huh?

JERRY (*Going to the phone and picking up the directory*) I'd better give General Thurman his ting-a-ling as per instructions.

MRS. JACOBY Before you ting-a-ling, Jerry, I want to tell you Mr. Asano is coming here.

ALICE (*Pleased*) Here?

JERRY When?

MRS. JACOBY Tonight. It's a Japanese custom called "go I to tea." [*Go-ai-sa-tsu.*]

ALICE What's that?

MRS. JACOBY According to Japanese etiquette, if you make a visit on somebody, he has to return the visit right back.

JERRY Why didn't he just bring you home?

MRS. JACOBY Because Mr. Asano's very formal about etiquette and, secondly, I wanted to give you a little chance to be prepared.

ALICE What'll we serve him?

MRS. JACOBY Tea. Mr. Asano's a very plain man, full of wisdom, and I'd like you to get to know him a little and you'll see what an unusual man he is. Don't laugh—he thinks I'm smart, too.

JERRY Wait till the boys in my shop hear that Mr. Asano's sweet on Mama.
   (*He returns to looking up the number.* ALICE *crosses above the table and examines the packages*)

121

MRS. JACOBY Then you wouldn't mind if I go with Mr. Asano throughout the winter to plays, concerts or national events?

ALICE Why not?
(*She has a box close to her face, examining it closely*)

JERRY Of course not, Mama. You don't have to ask.
(*He starts to dial*)

MRS. JACOBY In this country, when a man and a woman go to plays, and concerts and national events, it means they're keeping company.
(ALICE *slowly puts the box on the table.* JERRY *puts down the phone and slowly turns, not believing his ears*)

JERRY What did you say, Mama?

ALICE Jerry, I'm sure Mama's just using a phrase.

MRS. JACOBY No. When Mr. Asano says "keeping company," he means—"keeping company."

JERRY Certainly you don't take it seriously.

ALICE Mama *knows* it's impossible. Don't you, Mama?

JERRY What did you tell him?

MRS. JACOBY Mostly, I listened to a story about an emperor who married a lady of the court.

ALICE Married! Mama, you're a very smart woman. You know what such a marriage would mean. I don't have to tell you. You can't be considering it. You just can't.

MRS. JACOBY All I'm doing is thinking.

JERRY Mama, there's nothing to think about. I know what I'm talking about. I've been to lots of countries. I've seen a great deal of this sort of thing. At best, it's difficult. With you, Mama, it's ludicrous.
(*She looks at him*)

ALICE He means unsuitable, Mama. Not for a woman like you.

JERRY Mama, you're so bigoted you can't eat a piece of bacon. How are you going to marry a Japanese? Don't you realize—

MRS. JACOBY *Genug!*

ALICE I'm sure if you think it over—

MRS. JACOBY (*Rising—interrupting angrily*) I said *genug!* I mean *genug!* And if you forgot your Yiddish, that means enough!

JERRY Now just let me say this—

MRS. JACOBY You said already. You said "bigoted!"

ALICE   Mama, we'd never stand in the way of your remarrying if you wanted to—if the man were—
(*She falters*)

JERRY   I just want to point out a few facts. Do you understand what intermarriage means?

MRS. JACOBY   I'll discuss that with Mr. Asano—not you.

JERRY   Mama, you're deliberately evading the central question.

MRS. JACOBY   And the central question which aggravates you is that Mr. Asano is Japanese. (*He looks down*) In Brooklyn when Essie Rubin said she couldn't live with that element, you got very excited. You made a speech. Remember what you said? Because if you don't remember, I remember. You said, "If you want to stop prejudice, you've got to stop it in yourself." You forgot it, Jerry? (*He looks at her, then turns away*)—or maybe you changed your mind? (*She turns to* ALICE) And you, Alice? You agreed with Jerry.

ALICE   That was theoretical, Mama—on a broad social plane. It's different—

MRS. JACOBY   When it strikes home? Yes. And now, my dear children, I'd like to ask one simple question. Who's bigoted? (*There is a pause as they are unable to answer. Then the door buzzer sounds*) That must be Mr. Asano. So go answer the door, Jerry, and put a smile on your face. And don't stand there like all the pipes in the house just busted. And don't say one word to Mr. Asano—you hear? Not one word. Just go to the door and be pleasant.

(JERRY *goes to the door*)

JERRY (*Off*) Good evening, Mr. Asano.

MR. ASANO (*Off*) Good evening, Mr. Black.

JERRY (*Off*) Won't you come in, please?
(JERRY *enters, followed by* MR. ASANO)

MRS. JACOBY Good evening, Mr. Asano.

MR. ASANO (*Bowing to her*) Good evening. (*Bowing to* ALICE) Good evening, Mrs. Black. I'm delighted to see you again.

ALICE Good evening, Mr. Asano.

MR. ASANO (*Bowing slightly to* JERRY) Mr. Black.

JERRY (*Extending his hand*) Mr. Asano. (MR. ASANO *looks at* MRS. JACOBY—*then shakes* JERRY's *hand*) Won't you sit down, sir? (MR. ASANO *moves down to the arm chair and stands, waiting for the ladies to be seated.* MRS. JACOBY *sits on the sofa;* ALICE *sits on one of the chairs by the table.* MR. ASANO *then sits and* JERRY *sits on the other chair by the table. There is a long, awkward pause as they all sit erect, looking straight ahead, hands in laps. Then* JERRY *rises*) May I offer you a cigar, Mr. Asano.

MR. ASANO No, thank you. I do not smoke.

(JERRY *resumes his seat. There is another pause*)

MRS. JACOBY I was just telling the children what a lovely dinner I had at your house.

MR. ASANO I hope they will accept my hospitality. Perhaps Saturday evening. Unless, of course, Mr. Black, you feel it unsuitable during these negotiations.

JERRY We would be delighted to come, sir.

MR. ASANO You have not said anything, Mrs. Black.

(ALICE *starts to answer*)

MRS. JACOBY Alice never talks much.

MR. ASANO Nevertheless, I have the feeling there is something she would *like* to say. Please say it, Mrs. Black.

ALICE Mr. Asano, my mother has told me—well, of your conversation this evening.

MR. ASANO No doubt you were surprised.

ALICE Yes, I was. As a matter of fact, I was *more* than—

MRS. JACOBY That's enough, Alice.

MR. ASANO Please permit her to continue, Mrs. Jacoby.

ALICE (*She rises; the men rise*)   I don't quite know how to put it.

MR. ASANO   You do not approve.

ALICE   I'm certain if you talk to your own family, Mr. Asano, if you would take all the facts into account—

JERRY   I'm sure that upon deeper consideration, Mr. Asano, you will—

MR. ASANO   Mr. and Mrs. Black, I understand your views completely. I can even think of arguments that have not occurred to you because I am both a Buddhist and a Shintoist, making things far more complicated that you can *possibly* imagine. But any final decision must rest between your mother and myself. *We* have the maturity to weigh matters; you—have—not.

MRS. JACOBY (*Coming to the rescue*)   Alice, I think Mr. Asano would like a cup of tea.

MR. ASANO   It would be a pleasure.
     (ALICE *exits*)

MRS. JACOBY   Jerry—

JERRY   Yes, Mama.

MRS. JACOBY   Please get me a sweater or something. It's a little chilly in here.

JERRY Of course.

(*He follows* ALICE *off.* MR. ASANO *looks after them*)

MR. ASANO Do you usually keep your sweaters in the kitchen, Mrs. Jacoby?

MRS. JACOBY Please sit down, Mr. Asano.

(*He sits*)

MR. ASANO It is apparent that your children are agitated.

MRS. JACOBY That's putting it mildly. Did you speak to your daughter-in-law?

MR. ASANO I did, Mrs. Jacoby.

MRS. JACOBY And what did she say?

MR. ASANO Nothing. She would not dream of questioning my judgment.

MRS. JACOBY She wasn't shocked that you are considering keeping company with a Jewish woman.

MR. ASANO Mrs. Jacoby, my daughter-in-law is not aware of the theological differences existing in Caucasian society. If she has any objections, it is simply because you are white.

MRS. JACOBY I got the same argument from the opposite side.

MR. ASANO In view of that, have you come to a decision?

128

MRS. JACOBY Yes. (*She rises and crosses to him. He rises*) Mr. Asano, if keeping company means crossing the bridge, then it's no.

MR. ASANO You are acceding to your relatives' views?

MRS. JACOBY No.

MR. ASANO Then may I ask what prompted your decision?

MRS. JACOBY First, I'd like to tell you what did *not* prompt it. I don't care about gossip and I think we could work it out that I'm Orthodox and you're not. (*Smiling wryly*) I could even learn to make *sukiyaki* with kosher meat.

MR. ASANO But the answer is still no?

MRS. JACOBY Yes, it's no. And you know why? Because I've been weighing it pro and con. You don't want to marry me, Mr. Asano. You're lonely for your wife and somebody to talk to. You look at me and you see her. All right, she was Japanese and she wore a *kimono*. Tonight so did I.

MR. ASANO I saw a great deal more than that, Mrs. Jacoby.

MRS. JACOBY No, Mr. Asano. You're not over your mourning period. And neither am I. I'm very honored and very proud and deeply touched by what you said to me tonight. (*She turns away*) But you're not Sam.

129

MR. ASANO (*He crosses to her*) Mrs. Jacoby, there is something
I have left out of what I have said tonight. In my own way—
I love you.

(*She turns, he bows and leaves. The outside door closes.*
ALICE *and* JERRY *enter*)

MRS. JACOBY You can take the green look off your face. I told
him no. But not for *your* reasons—for my *own*—reasons you
didn't give me a chance to tell you.

ALICE What did he say to you, Mama?

MRS. JACOBY Only something for me to hear. You think it was
easy? You think it wasn't good to be treated with respect and
admired by a wonderful man? And courted like Papa courted
me long ago? It was. I can't lie. I had an evening in which
I was young again and it's over. But, at least, I have another
memory—maybe another regret. (ALICE *sits on the sofa beside
her*) And now, my dear children, I want you to get me a
ticket on the first airplane leaving tomorrow morning for
International Airport, New York, because I'm going home.

ALICE No, Mama. We'll do better.

MRS. JACOBY You did the best you could. It made no sense
for me to come and it makes no sense for me to stay. You'll
write me often and I'll write you back. What are you standing alone, Jerry? Come on in—the water's fine. (*He crosses,
takes her extended hand and sits beside her*) You're very
nice children—educated, sophisticated, pretty—

130

JERRY Mama, I'm more sophisticated than I was an hour ago, but I don't think I'm so pretty.

MRS. JACOBY To me you're pretty. And now all I hope for you is that you transcend—

ALICE Transcend?

MRS. JACOBY Yes. Transcend—and that together you achieve the serenity of the enlightened spirit.
(JERRY *and* ALICE *look puzzled*)

JERRY (*Smiling*) "The serenity of the enlightened spirit?" I never heard that in Hebrew school.

MRS. JACOBY How could you? It just so happens, Jerry, that what I have reference to is Zen Buddhism.

Curtain

Scene 2

The scene: MRS. JACOBY's *living room in Brooklyn. A few months later.*

At rise: The living room is the same except for a few souvenirs from Japan. A kakemono *hangs on the outside door and an oriental statue flanks the samovar on the sideboard. The table is covered with a white cloth and is set for dinner for two. In the center is a single yellow rose in a vase.*

ESSIE RUBIN *comes out of the kitchen, carrying two plates of gefülte fish. She puts them on the service plates and critically surveys the table. She calls toward the bedroom door which is open.*

MRS. RUBIN   Bertha! Would you like to lend my sterling silver fruit bowl for the center of the table?

MRS. JACOBY (*Off*)   No, Essie, it's just the way I want it.

MRS. RUBIN   That little flower looks very skimpy.

MRS. JACOBY (*Off*)   It's Moribana style.

MRS. RUBIN   Oh, another word you learned in Japan?

MRS. JACOBY (*Entering from bedroom, smoothing her new navy-blue dress*) No, another word I learned from the Japanese book of etiquette.

MRS. RUBIN Oh, Bertha, you look stunning!

MRS. JACOBY It's my twenty-nine-ninety-five number. (*She surveys the table*) I like how you fixed the fish, Essie, but you didn't put the horseradish on the lettuce.

MRS. RUBIN You only got red horseradish, Bertha. That's not for a formal dinner. I'll run down to Waldbaum's and get white.
(*She starts to the door*)

MRS. JACOBY Don't run! Mr. Asano will like the color. And besides you just want to get out of here to avoid meeting him.
(*She looks at her wrist watch and then crosses to peer out the window down into the street*)

MRS. RUBIN Frankly, Bertha, I'm a little embarrassed. Do I bow? Do I shake hands?

MRS. JACOBY You just act natural. (ESSIE *sits on sofa*) Essie?

ESSIE Hmmm?

MRS. JACOBY A lot of neighbors on the stoop. (ESSIE *shrugs and extends her hands in a helpless gesture*) What did you do? Send out a broadcast Mr. Asano was coming?

MRS. RUBIN I just told the super—

MRS. JACOBY It's a whole reception committee. Mrs. Rosensweig brought out her camp chair.

MRS. RUBIN You know, Bertha, you should have gotten in a maid. It's not too late. My cleaning woman is still in my apartment. She even has a little cap with a black bow!

MRS. JACOBY So let her keep the black bow. I don't have to show off for Mr. Asano. Sit, Essie.
    (*She goes to the sideboard for two candles*)

MRS. RUBIN You're showing off plenty with the dinner. What did you pay for the squabs?

MRS. JACOBY (*Places candles on the table*) I wouldn't be bankrupt.

MRS. RUBIN You know, Bertha—I don't think carrot *tsimmis* goes with squab.

MRS. JACOBY I've also got fresh peas with blanched almonds and potato puffs.

MRS. RUBIN (*Triumphantly*) But no salad!

MRS. JACOBY With an appetizer, fish, matzo ball soup, squab, vegetables and a noodle charlotte—a salad is not required.

MRS. RUBIN You know, Bertha, my daughter-in-law gave me such a thing last year you can make rosettes out of radishes and curl up celery and make cucumbers like little dolls. (*Starting for the door*) I'll go and make you some.

MRS. JACOBY (*Pointing to the sofa*) Essie, don't go and make. Sit.
(ESSIE *sits on the sofa.* MRS. JACOBY *goes to the sideboard for the tray on which are a wine decanter and glasses*)

MRS. JACOBY You decided on a trip, Essie?
(*She places the tray on the table*)

MRS. RUBIN Not yet. It's between Lakewood and the Virgin Islands.

MRS. JACOBY That's some between. (*The door buzzer sounds. They both react*) Essie. Be calm. (*She opens the door.* MR. ASANO *is there.* ESSIE *rises uncertainly*) Mr. Asano!

MR. ASANO Mrs. Jacoby!

MRS. JACOBY Please come in and excuse the disorder of my house. (*He enters. He is wearing a coat and carries his hat*) Did you have a hard time getting here?

MR. ASANO No. I remember you instructed me to take the Lexington Express to Franklin Avenue and then change to a New Lots train and debark at Kingston Avenue. After due consideration, I took a taxi.

MRS. JACOBY   I should have suggested that in the first place. I'd like you to meet my friend, Mrs. Rubin. Essie, this is Mr. Asano of Tokyo, Japan.

MR. ASANO   I am honored.

MRS. RUBIN   Likewise. Did you have a nice trip from Japan?

MR. ASANO   Oh yes. Excellent. Your DC-7C is a most remarkable plane.

MRS. RUBIN   Well, if you'll excuse me, I have to go and get dressed. I'm going over to someone's house for a little pot-luck, and then we'll watch "Person to Person."

MRS. JACOBY   That's a television program.

MR. ASANO   I hope you enjoy it, Mrs. Rubin.

MRS. RUBIN   Thank you. Very pleased to have made your acquaintance, Mr. Asano. I hope to have the pleasure again.

MR. ASANO   Likewise.

MRS. RUBIN   (*She looks at him, then at* MRS. JACOBY *and then back at him. Then, gaily, she makes a sweeping bow*)   Sayonara!
    (*She exits*)

MRS. JACOBY   She is so flustered meeting you, Mr. Asano.

MR. ASANO It was charming of her to say, "*Sayonara*."

MRS. JACOBY (*Taking his coat*) It was charming of you to call me.

MR. ASANO It was charming of you to invite me to dinner.

MRS. JACOBY And it was charming— There must be another way to start a sentence. Please sit down. (*She places his coat on a chair*) I was so excited when you called—I had so many questions to ask, I didn't ask one. So what brings you to this neck of the woods?
     (*She sits on the sofa. He sits beside her*)

MR. ASANO A variety of matters.

MRS. JACOBY Business?

MR. ASANO Only incidentally.

MRS. JACOBY I understand that you signed a very nice treaty.

MR. ASANO A tentative agreement for a short period. You'll be pleased to know it involves some degree of diversification.

MRS. JACOBY Are you happy with it?

MR. ASANO No, not particularly. But I *am* particularly happy to see you again.

MRS. JACOBY   And I am also happy to see you.

MR. ASANO   For a long period, my government has been asking me to accept a seat with our delegation to the United Nations. I have agreed.

MRS. JACOBY   Congratulations.

MR. ASANO   I shall spend a great deal of time here in New York, in that great glass building.

MRS. JACOBY   That will be very nice.

MR. ASANO   Mrs. Jacoby, I was present at a dinner in Tokyo at the Imperial Hotel last week in honor of Mr. Fujiyama. He is not a mountain, Mrs. Jacoby, but an important official. Your government was represented by your son-in-law.

MRS. JACOBY   Did Jerry do well?

MR. ASANO   Very well, indeed. He commenced his speech in Japanese—not *good* Japanese, but Japanese—which we all took as a great compliment.

MRS. JACOBY   Was my daughter also at the dinner?

MR. ASANO   Oh, yes, looking lovely in a deep-red dress. Many of my colleagues commented on how attractive she was. Her eyes were shining.

138

MRS. JACOBY That's because I'm going to be a grandmother.

MR. ASANO Oh, that is splendid news!

MRS. JACOBY The best news I ever had. Now, if you'll excuse me, I'll just get my dinner in motion.
     (*She rises and goes into the kitchen, leaving the door open. He rises, watches her go and then he moves above the sofa. He suddenly smiles, remembering "baby blue," places both hands on the back of it and looks it over carefully. He then turns and sees the samovar on the sideboard above the sofa*)

MR. ASANO What a lovely samovar.

MRS. JACOBY (*Off*) It belonged to my grandmother.

MR. ASANO (*He looks at the oval-framed pictures above the breakfront*) Is this your grandmother's portrait on the wall?

MRS. JACOBY (*Off*) No, my mother's. And the gentleman with the beard is my father.

MR. ASANO He has a distinguished look. (*He next looks at the pictures of Sam and David Jacoby.* MRS. JACOBY *enters with a tray of canapés*) This is your husband and your son?

MRS. JACOBY Yes.

MR. ASANO   The son looks like the father. Isn't it curious—they both look like you.

MRS. JACOBY   I never noticed. Now, will you sit to my table, please. (*He moves to the chair and waits for her to be seated*) No, don't wait for me, Mr. Asano. I'll be jumping up and down, so make yourself comfortable.

MR. ASANO   I'm most comfortable. Your house has a warm feeling. (*They sit*) It is homelike.

MRS. JACOBY   Thank you. I hope you like chopped liver.

MR. ASANO (*He tastes some*)   Excellent. It tastes like bean-jam buns. (*Looking at the plate before him*) What is this, Mrs. Jacoby?

MRS. JACOBY   That's gefülte fish. It's made of all different kinds of fish to represent all the oceans and lakes. We eat it on holidays—festivals—and Friday nights. Oh! I didn't light the candles.

   (*She rises and goes to the sideboard for a scarf and matches*)

MR. ASANO (*Also rising*)   May I be of some help?

MRS. JACOBY   No, the lady of the house lights the Sabbath candles. (*She returns to stand above the table*) I waited for you. I thought you might like to see how we observe.

MR. ASANO I shall be most interested.

(She covers her head with the scarf, lights the candles, stretches out her hands. She intones a prayer. MR. ASANO *watches with respectful interest. She removes her scarf)*

MRS. JACOBY That's all there is to it. I just said, "Praised be Thou, O, Lord, our God, King of the Universe, Who has sanctified us by Thy commandments and has instructed us to kindle the Sabbath lights. Amen."

MR. ASANO Amen.

(She places her scarf on the breakfront)

MRS. JACOBY And now we have a little blackberry wine.

(She pours the wine, hands him a glass and takes one for herself. They move back to their chairs)

MR. ASANO Mrs. Jacoby, I do not see my wife in you now. I am quite recovered from my mourning period.

MRS. JACOBY *(Sitting)* It takes time, doesn't it? It takes a little longer for women than for men.

MR. ASANO Yes. indeed. *(He sits. They place their napkins on their laps)* I see that there are many plays in New York— and a series of concerts at Carnegie Hall.

MRS. JACOBY And soon it will be Thanksgiving.

MR. ASANO One of your important national events. I hope we may celebrate it together, Mrs. Jacoby.

MRS. JACOBY For Thanksgiving you'll come to my house. (*They raise their wine glasses*) *Kompai*, Mr. Asano.

MR. ASANO *L'chayim*, Mrs. Jacoby.

Curtain

A